Be Encouraged

Be Encouraged

100 MESSAGES OF HOPE AND HEALING

Rev. Robin Harris Kimbrough

BE ENCOURAGED: 100 MESSAGES OF HOPE AND HEALING
COPYRIGHT @ 2015: Rev. Robin Harris Kimbrough

SCRIPTURE QUOTATIONS ARE TAKEN FROM THE NEW REVISED STANDARD VERSION.

ISBN-13: 9780975553008
ISBN-10: 0975553003
All rights reserved.

COVER ILLUSTRATION BY LOGO MY LOGO
MANUFACTURED IN THE UNITED STATES OF AMERICA

DEDICATION

To Elizabeth—
I admire you so much. Your hard work, focus, diligence, and love for God inspire and encourage me every day as a mother. I have had the privilege to watch you grow into a beautiful young lady.
You are Batman; I am Robin.

Be encouraged.

To Adric, Jr.—
I have watched you grow into a fine young man. I am encouraged to see you as leader and advocate for the community. Your love for golf inspires me. You have learned and played this game with limited resources.
Yet, you still manage to be on top.

Be encouraged.

Foreword

This book is a collection of selected condensed sermons written for the *Nashville Pride*, a local urban newspaper in Nashville, Tennessee. I have contributed to the paper as a columnist since 2003. Mrs. Henrietta Harbison, a loyal reader of the *Nashville Pride*, inspired me to begin this project because she had collected my sermons since I started to write for the paper. Over the years, she has clipped hundreds of these reflections and pasted them in her special family photo album. While Mrs. Harbison read these sermons, my congregation at Scott United Methodist Church, in Shelbyville, Tennessee, heard them preached.

Over the past 15 years, I have gone through both discouraging and exhilarating moments. I have married and divorced and mothered two great children, Elizabeth and Adric. These years have allowed me to explore my calling to kingdom building as a pastor, chaplain, writer and attorney. I have changed for the better; I am not the same.

We all get discouraged for many reasons, especially when we are embarking on a project like writing a book. Since graduating from Vanderbilt Divinity School, I have had a desire to write. For many years, I wrote curriculum for Abingdon Press. Yet, the urge to write a book remained. Now, here it is – 15 years later. I thought I had wasted time on hurt, pain and other people. Then, I realized that God has an appointed time for everything.

I am grateful to the 20 people who served as focus group members or volunteer editors. Their faith in me helped me to make it over the finish line. I could not let them down. Most importantly, my faith in God and the power of Jesus Christ prepared and enabled me to complete this work and embark upon future writing endeavors.

Be Encouraged is my faith journey. I share personal pain, joy and life lessons learned from my children. God has a way of introducing us to books and people to keep us encouraged. I hope that *Be Encouraged* inspires you and brings you hope. Read and be encouraged!

Be encouraged!

All things are possible
Mark 10:27

Preface

Most of us are familiar with the parables of Jesus. From the story of the Good Samaritan, we learn about compassion. The Pharisee and the Publican account teaches us about humility. And the parable of the Prodigal Son imparts important truths about forgiveness and restoration.

Much as Jesus told simple stories to illustrate moral or spiritual values, the Rev. Robin Harris Kimbrough opens a window to her soul to share lessons learned – and lessons taught.

I started reading Rev. Kimbrough's weekly columns more than ten years ago. Her interesting, endearing stories reference life experiences, everyday common sense and God's holy Word. As I read, I thought of my own family. I put the saved stories next to memorable family member's photos because the readings – as I saw them – related to their character and/or life experiences. They continue to give me encouragement for everything important in my life.

I can truly say that Rev. Kimbrough's writings have a biblical tone, which inspires and reminds me, always, to express my love to God, family and friends. They are a source of help and strength for me.

In the Scriptures, Jesus taught life lessons through parables and the struggles and choices of the people he encountered. Through Rev. Kimbrough's reflections of faith, hope and love, Jesus continues this work. I pray these readings will inspire you as they inspire me.

Henrietta Harbison

Table of Contents

Become · 1

Be Assured · 71

Be Encouraged · 139

Become

Become

A Heart for God	3
All Talk, No Action	5
An Escape Plan	7
Back to the Basics	9
Beware of the Dogs	11
Bitter Can Become Better	13
Dealing with Temptation	15
Destined to Be a Butterfly	17
Don't Let Anger Get the Best of You	19
Don't Look Back	21
Forgive Yourself	23
Get Out of the Way	25
God Has Plans for You	27
Help Is on the Way!	29
I'm Getting Better	31
Jesus Is Worth the Wait	33
Life is a Climb	35
Life Is Too Short	37
Live Through It!	39
Peter Decided to Follow Jesus	41
Physically Fit for Spiritual Fitness	43
Rebuild Me	45
Rightly Proclaiming the Word of Truth	47
Send Me!	49
Stand, Take Up Your Mat and Walk	51
Strive for Your Goals	53
Through the Roof	55
Too Close	57
Turn the Other Cheek	59
What Do You Have to Fear?	61
What Must I do to Be Saved?	63
You Are Worth Saving	65
You Look Better When You Smile	67

We must love God with our hearts.

A Heart for God

Traditionally, Valentine's Day is devoted to celebrating the romantic love of one's life. Some have expanded the celebration to include children and other significant people in their lives. The Valentine's Day symbol is a red heart. Biologically, the heart is the organ that keeps us alive. If our heart stops beating, there is a strong possibility that we have passed on to the other side. When we figuratively give someone our heart, we are giving them our lives and that is love. This is the heart we must have for God.

David, King Saul's replacement, had a heart for God. "But now your kingdom will not continue; the Lord has sought out a man after his own heart; and the Lord has appointed him to be ruler over his people, because you have not kept what the Lord commanded you" (1 Samuel 13:14).

Like David, we must have a heart for God. We must love God with our hearts. If our heart is not in something, no matter how much we try or have the skills to do it, it will not work out, and we will be unhappy doing it.

Remember the Tin Man from the Wizard of Oz, who thought he needed a heart when in fact his compassion for Dorothy and his companions revealed he already had a big heart. He found out that having a heart is more than having a muscle to pump blood through his veins. This heart cannot come from a wizard and it does not have four chambers; it comes from having a heart for God.

We have to have heart for what we do. My son, Adric, plays golf, and he has a heart for the game. He practices for hours in the rain and extreme cold; he wants to play golf more than eating lunch. Adric gets more joy out of playing golf than winning golf tournaments. When we have a heart for God, we get more joy out of being in a relationship with him than seeing what we can get out of him, and we will worship him in all types of weather.

When we have a heart for God, whatever we do becomes more about God than what we personally gain. It means showing compassion for humanity. We must have a heart for the poor, marginalized communities, others who may look different, and those who do not have a heart for us. When we open our hearts in this way, the heart will break. We will have disappointments, things may not go our way, challenges will arise and we will be tempted to lose heart. But God is able to mend a broken heart.

God knows that our heart is critical to our spiritual living. God's love keeps our hearts beating and open to everything God has in store for us.

Have a heart for God.

Feeding the hungry, visiting the sick, clothing the naked, visiting people or welcoming the stranger cover many of the world's needs.

All Talk, No Action

Matthew devotes his 25th chapter to Jesus' discourse on the Kingdom of God and the end times. Jesus shares three parables. The first involves ten virgins, five wise and five foolish. He teaches that being wise means being ready for Jesus who may come at any time. The foolish are not prepared for his coming because they come with lamps, but no oil.

The second parable is about three men who receive talents from their master. Jesus reveals that through God's grace, we have been given certain gifts to multiply and bring back to God. How we use what God has given us is not to be about us; it's about giving him the glory. When we step out on faith, God trusts us with more. When we fail to work with the things God has given us, we end up with nothing.

The last parable expands on the discussion of the Kingdom of God and what it takes to be saved. Jesus reemphasizes that our faith requires us to act. As revealed in Matthew, many people say they are saved, but they are not. Jesus distinguishes two groups of people – those who talk and those who act on what they say. Believing in Jesus and confessing Christ as Lord requires more than talk; it requires action. We act because we are saved, not to be saved. Our actions reflect our love for God and our belief in Jesus Christ. Jesus offers ideas about what kind of action exemplifies our belief and confession in Christ: feeding the hungry, visiting the sick, clothing the naked, visiting people in prison and welcoming the stranger. Jesus says, "Just as you did it to one of the least of these who are members of my family, you did it to me" (Matthew 25:40b).

When we experience salvation, we should instinctively want to serve God. Feeding the hungry, visiting the sick, clothing the naked, visiting people, and welcoming the stranger cover many of the world's needs. When we respond to God's grace, it should move us to serve him. Serving others is serving God. Jesus did not die for us to do a lot of talking; he wants us to act.

When Jesus is Lord over our lives, faith is more than a noun; it is a verb. When we put our faith into action, God's love becomes active in our lives and the lives of others. The truth is the world would be a better place if we were more action than talk. The best sermon any of us will preach will be the one we live. Serving the Lord will pay off after a while.

No matter how trapped we feel in our circumstances – problems, negative people or confusion, there is always a way of escape.

An Escape Plan

As a child, I enjoyed finding my way through mazes – the more challenging the better. The maze provides a starting point, and the challenge becomes finding the way out – the escape—through many routes leading to dead-ends.

Life can be like a maze. We find ourselves at a starting point, and we are left with the task of finding the way out. Like in a maze puzzle, we may see the exit, but it is hard to figure out how to go through the twists and turns to find the route to the exit. Although this is frustrating, the good news is that there is a way out. There is a way of escape.

Paul, who once persecuted Christians, faced his own persecutions as a Christian. The newly converted Saul often found himself risking his life for his profession of faith in Jesus Christ. On one occasion, Paul had to remain trapped in the city, because there were people plotting to kill him. "After some time had passed, the Jews plotted to kill him, but their plot became known to Saul. They were watching the gates day and night so that they might kill him; but his disciples took him by night and let him down through an opening in the wall, lowering him in a basket" (Acts 9:23-25).

The disciples and Paul came up with an escape plan. We learn through Paul's situation that God always provides a way of escape. No matter how trapped we feel in our circumstances – problems, negative people or confusion, there is always a way of escape. When we find ourselves in situations in which the walls feel as if they are closing in on us, we must think creatively on what God wants us to do and on God's plan for our escape.

Many of us remain in our traps because we refuse to think outside the box. We limit God to our own understanding of what we need to be delivered from or how to escape our situation. We do not have to be in the maze because God has given us the way out. We just need faith to find it. As we strategize about our escape plans, let us not limit God, but be open to baskets, sheets, ropes and people to help us because they are all a part of God's escape plan. The Lord will make a way somehow.

We need to get back to the basics and ask ourselves how we would want to be treated, and give that same treatment to someone else.

Back to the Basics

One of the first concepts we learn in math is addition. Addition is a fundamental concept in math upon which more complicated operations are built. Math builds on concepts, and without the basic knowledge of rules and equations, learning the advanced topics would prove to be a struggle and almost impossible to learn. Our Christian journey is very similar. There are basic concepts that we need to learn and master before moving on to more advanced topics on our spiritual walk. As we move forward in learning and maturing in God, we often forget about the basics, and we end up in a situation in which we need to know the basics.

In Jesus' Sermon on the Mount, Jesus provides the basics of Christian living. One of the basic concepts he teaches is love and how to treat one another. It is set forth in the Golden Rule: "Therefore, whatever you want people to do to you, do also to them, for this is the Law and the Prophets" (Matthew 7:12).

How many of us have yelled at someone because the person yelled at us? How many of us have refused to help someone move or give them a ride because it was out of our way? How many of us have left the waiter a less than fifteen percent tip or no tip at all? How many of us have ignored someone in need? We need to get back to the basics and ask ourselves how we would want to be treated, and give that same treatment to someone else.

Rather than responding to our instinctive reaction to make someone hurt like we hurt or withholding resources from someone we feel does not deserve them, we need to get back to the basics doing unto others as we would like to have done unto us. If we as God's children would get back to this basic rule of living, we would be able to approach more advanced issues with less complicated methods. We need to get back to the basics like love, forgiveness, and compassion because everything else builds upon these blocks. If we are willing to share love with others, we will receive love in return. If we get back to the basics, we will live in a world where all lives matter.

Let's get back to the basics.

George Clinton said it best, "Ain't nothing but the dog in me." Paul taught that if we get this dog under control, we can make other dogs kneel, sit and roll over.

Beware of the Dogs

Paul's letter to the church at Philippi warned the church against dogs. The dogs to which Paul referred were not pit bulls, poodles, or wiener dogs. These dogs were spirits. Paul's warning holds true for us today: "Beware of the dogs, beware of the evil workers, beware of those who mutilate the flesh!" (Philippians 3:2). Paul cautioned against spirits that seek to judge and challenge the church. Because the church at Philippi focused on faith in Jesus Christ and striving to do the right thing, Paul wanted to give them a stern warning so the members would remain steadfast. Regardless of how strong we think we are, our faith and willingness to do God's will is always in jeopardy.

Beware of the dogs. They nip at our heels, sniff us out and lick us with the intent to bite us. While we journey toward divine destiny, these dogs run loose, bark at us and put so much fear in our hearts that we are frightened to do God's will and work. These dogs travel in packs with nothing better to do than conspire and destroy us. We have to realize that these dogs exist so beware. Otherwise, we will allow these evil workers to have their way with us. These evil workers are in the church, the workplace and even our families.

Some dogs look good on the outside, but they are not concerned with Christian living. These dogs are often difficult to spot because they are clean, well-kept dogs. They are "physically circumcised," but there is no change on the inside. They have religion, but they have no relationship with God. They are good at convincing believers that they are saved because of what they wear, their knowledge of the Bible, and their regular attendance at church. Beware! Salvation takes place in the heart.

Finally, there is the dog – our flesh – that dwells inside us. It constantly yelps. We struggle with keeping it on a leash or putting it back on a leash. George Clinton said it best, "Ain't nothing but the dog in me." Paul taught that if we get this dog under control, we can make other dogs kneel, sit and roll over. If that dog inside us is out of control, everything around us will be out of control. We cannot put this dog on a leash by ourselves; we need a dogcatcher. The dogcatcher is grace. Grace provides us with self-control and discipline.

If we respond to God's grace, all of these dogs will leave our presence whimpering, knowing that they have no authority over us.

Beware of the dogs!

Life can be tough to swallow like the bitter waters of Marah, but if we put our faith in God, these challenges can make us better.

Bitter Can Become Better

Life can leave a bitter taste in our mouths. A broken heart, financial troubles, hurt feelings or our own sinfulness can make us bitter. Whatever it is, we can get better.

God finally answered the Israelites cries for deliverance from Egypt, a place where they suffered as slaves for hundreds of years. The Egyptian Pharaoh chased the Israelites, but God destroyed Pharaoh's army and the Israelites were able to make a clean get-away. After escaping Pharaoh's army, they wandered for three days looking for water. Faced with dehydration and the frustration of having left Egypt where there was plenty of water, they were desperate. They found a body of water named Marah. Imagine their joy when they discovered the water, and then as they drank with anticipation of satisfying their thirst, only to have tasted bitter, undrinkable water. They complained to Moses. Although they witnessed the miracle of Pharaoh's army drowning in the Red Sea, while they crossed safely, they still were hopeless and upset over this situation. God told Moses to throw a piece of wood into the water and the water turned from bitter to sweet (Exodus 15:22-25).

Life can be tough to swallow like the bitter waters of Marah, but if we put our faith in God, these challenges can make us better. If we allow the challenges before us to strengthen us and shape us into what God intends, we will become better. God doesn't mean for bad things to happen to us, but God's will is to allow these situations to increase our faith and make us better to fulfill God's plan for our lives.

We must participate in our process of going from bitter to better. As God instructed Moses, we must throw a log into our bitter waters. Our log is God's grace, which makes any bitter situation sweet. It is up to us to allow the grace of God to bring out who we truly are in God. Instead of living with bitterness, we must have a desire and faith to become better. Believe it. Bitter can become better. When my children were smaller and they had a cut or some other type of injury, a Band-Aid and a kiss would make it all better. As they have grown older and experienced the pains of life, they have learned that they need more. They need the grace of God to turn their bitter into sweet. Bitter can become better.

Temptation can disguise itself as something that appears to be what is best for us, when in actuality it is a trap.

Dealing with Temptation

The truth is we are tempted to do things that we know we should not do. We struggle with eating that extra piece of pie, or enjoying the fried chicken rather than selecting the baked option. These choices are not so bad, but just imagine the temptation of using drugs, smoking, drinking alcohol, gossiping, and other behaviors that we may not actually do, but the thought of doing them runs through our minds. We need encouragement to resist temptation.

In the letter of James, he gives us some helpful tips on how to deal with temptation. James writes, "When tempted, no one should say, 'God is tempting me.' For God cannot be tempted by evil, nor does he tempt anyone; but each person is tempted when they are dragged away by their own evil desire and enticed. Then, after desire has conceived, it gives birth to sin; and sin, when it is full-grown, gives birth to death. Don't be deceived, my dear brothers and sisters." (James 1:13-16) We should expect temptation. We all will face temptation. If someone says that they have never been faced with temptation, they are not human.

We must realize that God is not the source of our temptation, but the devil, and the devil does it by setting traps for us. We have to be careful of the bait Satan uses to lure us into traps. Temptation can disguise itself as something that appears to be what is best for us, when in actuality it is a trap. How many of us have been disappointed over a relationship or job because after making so many sacrifices to make it work, we find out that it was a trap. A mouse gets caught in a trap, because of his greed for cheese.

He does not realize he is trapped until he is unable to get his leg out of the clip. Our desires, too, can get us trapped. This is why we must keep our focus on God. Through God's grace we can get out of these traps.

Let us not be deceived by temptation. The truth is we can resist it, and we can receive redemption from it. There is a car insurance commercial in which individuals make some outrageous choices resulting in bad accidents. The jingle reminds us that we are human, and that we are born to make mistakes. This is why we must rely on Jesus Christ, who is more than human, to help and encourage us to overcome temptation and to be delivered from it. This is how to deal with temptation.

If we are willing to allow the challenges put before us to strengthen us and shape us into what God intends, we will become beautiful butterflies.

Destined to Be a Butterfly

In the spring, leaves appear on the trees, flowers bloom, temperatures rise, rain falls and lawn mowers whirr. As the seasons go through cycles of growth and renewal so do we as humans, especially those who believe in Jesus Christ. Just as spring awakens the things in the earth that were dead and dormant, when we are born again in the Spirit, we experience a reawakening in our lives. We become new. Paul proclaims, "If anyone is in Christ, there is a new creation: everything old has passed away; see, everything has become new!" (2 Corinthians 5:17). We learn from this text that once we are in Christ, God intends for us to become new creatures – to change and become something brand new.

One of my favorite springtime insects is the caterpillar. Once it emerges from the cocoon, it turns from an ugly worm into a beautiful butterfly. But first, the caterpillar must experience a metamorphosis – a change. Our lifecycles as Christians are similar to that of the caterpillar. As Christians, we must go through a metamorphosis to walk into the destiny God has for us.

The most dangerous time for the butterfly is when it is a caterpillar. At this stage, it is vulnerable to the environment, including starvation, dehydration and predators, including children who like to catch them. Those surviving caterpillars undergo another metamorphosis to become a butterfly. They must shed their exoskeletons. After this process, the ugly worm emerges as a beautiful butterfly.

When we choose to follow Christ, we shed our old selves and become beautiful butterflies – new creatures in Christ. This is what Paul means when he says that old things pass away. Our exoskeletons disappear when we are born of the water and the Spirit. This transformation enables us to fly into our destinies as beautiful butterflies, to become something new and to do some things new.

Like the caterpillar, we must survive our environments to change into the new creatures God has destined us to be through Jesus Christ. If we are willing to allow the challenges put before us to strengthen us and shape us into what God intends, we will become beautiful butterflies.

You are a butterfly!

Angry people often take out their frustrations on people with whom they are close or those who have found favor in areas in which they feel rejected.

Don't Let Anger Get the Best of You

Many people walk around angry with God, themselves, family members, and even the world. Anger will get the best of anyone if the person lacks self-control. The sin is not in getting angry, the sin is when we let it get the best of us.

God gave Cain this very same warning when God found favor with Abel's offering over Cain's in Genesis 4. The brothers, Cain and Abel, both gave God an offering. Abel gave God the firstlings of his flock, and Cain gave God some fruit from the ground. Although the Scripture indicates that Abel gave the firstlings from his flock, scholars suggest that this reference does not mean that Abel's offering was any better than Cain's. In fact, there was no real difference in the value of the two offerings.

Cain could have congratulated Abel, but he chose to be hurt and angry. God admonished him. "Why are you angry, and why has your countenance fallen? If you do well, will you not be accepted? And if you do not do well, sin is lurking at the door; its desire is for you, but you must master it" (Genesis 4:6b-7).

Although God warned Cain against the power of his anger, he was too angry and hurt to listen. Cain was not upset with Abel; he was really mad at God. Instead of working out his anger and pain with God and presenting a more acceptable offering, he decided to eliminate the competition by murdering Abel, who had nothing to do with God's decision.

Angry people often take out their frustrations on people with whom they are close or those who have found favor in areas in which they feel rejected. Failure to cool off often leads one down the path of self-destruction and rage. According to Jesus, holding onto anger, even if we do not kill Abel, is just as bad as murder. We need to learn to kiss and make up, live and learn, agree to disagree, rejoice and praise, as well as forgive and forget.

Don't let anger get the best of you.

We need to keep moving, stop dwelling on the past and look forward with great expectation.

Don't Look Back

Many of us cannot move forward to the best that God has in store for us because we keep looking back and holding on to things that no longer matter. When God delivers us from people, things and situations, we must keep moving forward. We often look back because we get discouraged and become nostalgic over what we have left behind rather than trusting God and knowing that something better lies ahead. God has seen many of us out of destructive and sinful situations, including addictions, unhealthy relationships and dead-end jobs. But we must not look back.

We learn from the destruction of Sodom and Gomorrah that looking back can keep us from moving forward. God wanted to destroy Sodom and Gomorrah because everyone seemed to have turned away from God. Abraham intervened on behalf of the cities, and pleaded with God not to do it. God eventually decided to destroy Sodom and Gomorrah, and to permit Lot and his family to leave before he set the cities on fire. On the way out, the angel warned Lot's family not to look back. "But Lot's wife, behind him, looked back, and she became a pillar of salt" (Genesis 19:26).

As God delivers us from situations that are about to catch on fire, God tells us not to look back. Resisting our nature to look back is difficult. We are curious. While driving east on the interstate, we look back, stalling traffic, because we want to see the accident headed west. We need God's grace to focus our attention on what lies ahead: victory and prosperity.

If we want to participate in the blessings God has in store for us, we cannot look back to curses, people, and other destruction from which God has delivered us. Looking back can have fatal consequences. If we do not look forward and trust in God's will for our lives, we could turn into a pillar of salt. Dreams, hopes and goals turn into pillars of salt in our lives because we keep looking back on what we once were, what happened before and what is going on behind us. We need to keep moving, stop dwelling on the past and look forward with great expectation.

Don't look back!

When we sin, we must seek forgiveness from Jesus Christ and have faith in knowing our sins are forgiven.

Forgive Yourself

We have all heard, "When you fall off your horse, get back on it." This saying is easier said than done. Many people fall off their horses and have no intentions of getting back on them. Those who are seeking a way out of guilt and shame, should know that they will fall off their horses, they will make mistakes, but there is always an opportunity to remount and ride.

Paul shares the awesome truth about what it means to be in relationship with Jesus Christ: "There is therefore now no condemnation for those who are in Christ Jesus" (Romans 8:1). Many people who walk after the Spirit, devoutly read the Bible, attend church and Sunday school regularly live in self-condemnation. They live with feelings of guilt and shame, rather than accepting God's forgiveness through Christ Jesus. They beat themselves up for things that happened years ago.

When people live with self-condemnation, they cannot actualize the full potential of who they are in Christ. They spend more time finding reasons and excuses for not accepting God's blessings for them and passing these blessings to people whom they feel are more deserving. When opportunity knocks, they do not answer because they allow the guilt of their past to control their destiny.

When we sin, we must seek forgiveness from Jesus Christ and have faith in knowing our sins are forgiven. With this belief, we can truly live free of condemnation. We need to forgive ourselves so that we can improve ourselves. After playing a bad hole of golf, my son, Adric, does not let that keep him from playing the next holes better. In the same way, we cannot allow our mistakes to keep us from moving forward into something better. We cannot become who God wants us to be if we live under the mantle of condemnation.

We must accept that we will make mistakes, and forgive ourselves. God holds us guiltless through the blood of Jesus Christ and frees us from sin and the negative effects of sin. Why live enslaved to guilt, shame and other shackles, when there is abundant life in Christ Jesus? Through the blood of Jesus, we are reconciled with God in newness of life.

Get back on the horse; forgive yourself.

Emotions like fear, anger, insecurity, doubt and pride and a false belief that we know more than God get in the way of our blessings.

Get Out of the Way

One of the biggest frustrations occurs when something or someone blocks our progress. From traffic jams to fallen trees to jealous people, we know how frustrating it is when things and situations get in our way.

We easily recognize the obstacles standing on the outside of us, but we often overlook the biggest obstacle in our way – self! Naaman, a "mighty warrior," who also had leprosy, had this problem. He wanted to get rid of his leprosy, but he did not want to get out of the way. Naaman's servant advised him that a prophet in Israel had the power to heal him. Rather than seeking out the prophet, Naaman sought out the king of Israel to heal him. The king of Israel tore his clothes, thinking that the intent was to start a war. "Am I God, to give death or life, that this man sends word to me to cure a man of his leprosy? Just look and see how he is trying to pick a quarrel with me" (2 Kings 5:7). Naaman learned quickly that his problem required divine intervention.

Elisha, the man of God, got involved. Rather than meeting personally with Naaman, Elisha sent him instructions to dip in the Jordan seven times to get rid of the leprosy. Frustrated that Elisha did not meet with him personally and insulted that Elisha did not select a cleaner river, Naaman got upset and decided not to do anything. Naaman blocked his own way. The servants responded to Naaman's rage with these words, "Father, if the prophet had commanded you to do something difficult, would you not have done it? How much more, when all he said to you was, 'Wash, and be clean'?" (2 Kings 5:13).

Naaman dipped seven times in the Jordan, and he came out with skin like a baby. We are so much like Naaman. God tells us how to get rid of our leprosy – to work a miracle in our lives – but we question and criticize the instructions and stomp our feet and pout because we still have leprosy.

We cannot blame others for standing in our way. Emotions like fear, anger, insecurity, doubt and pride and a false belief that we know more than God get in the way of our blessings. We have the power to get rid of the leprosy, to go to the next level, to do something that requires a miracle if we are willing to do it God's way. When we get self out of the way and let the leprosy meet the water, we can go beyond expecting a miracle to becoming the miracle. So, get out of the way!

God will help us to see that this is not the plan for hope and good he has for us. This is why rejection is God's protection and redirection.

God Has Plans for You

One of the most frustrating, difficult and challenging tasks for people who seek to live holy and godly lives is discerning God's plan and purpose for their lives. Our personal desires, fears, and the expectations of others often cloud our ability to figure out God's plan for our lives. God will take aggressive steps to get us on back on track. The Holy Spirit constantly tries to redirect us towards God's purpose and plan.

Human nature can convince us that everything should go our way, and that anything outside of what we want for our lives is not a good plan. This line of thinking engages us in a constant struggle with our plans and God's plans. To overcome this dilemma, we must believe that God wants and knows what is best for each of us.

During a time when the Israelites needed direction and hope, God spoke through the prophet, Jeremiah, to let them know that God had plans for them, even though they were captive in Babylon. God told the Israelites, "For surely I know the plans I have for you, says the Lord, plans for your welfare and not for harm, to give you a future with hope. Then when you call upon me and come and pray to me, I will hear you. When you search for me, you will find me; if you seek me with all your heart, I will let you find me, says the Lord" (Jeremiah 29:11-14a).

Like the Israelites, we may be in a place of captivity. We may even think that captivity is God's ultimate plan for our lives. On the contrary, God's plans for us are not to harm us, but for hope and good. If we ever find ourselves at the crossroads of life wandering if we are in God's will, we should ask ourselves whether this decision will bring us harm or good. If the decision brings harm, it is not in God's plan for us. Often, that it is hard to accept that a choice we want to make is not part of God's plans. We may find ourselves attracted to someone, but if we were honest with ourselves, we know that the relationship would cause more harm than good. This is also true when we are deciding to choose a job, to go out to the movies, to hang out with friends, or doing anything else. God has plans for us, and they are for hope.

We must put our trust in God's plan and desire for our lives. God knows what is better for us than we do for ourselves. God grieves when we allow other people to make plans for us who do not have our best interest at heart. God will help us to see that this is not the plan for hope and good he has for us. This is why rejection is God's protection and redirection.

God has plans for you – plans of peace and hope.

No matter how far we have strayed and how lost we are in the wilderness of life, help is on the way!

Help Is on the Way!

The parable of the lost sheep, the first in the series of three parables about someone who lost something, is a reminder that when we are lost and alone, Jesus will leave ninety-nine and come looking for us. Before Jesus told the parable, the Pharisees and the scribes criticized Jesus because he associated with sinners. After he told the parable, Jesus explained, "Just so, I tell you, there will be more joy in heaven over one sinner who repents than over ninety-nine righteous persons who need no repentance" (Luke 15:4-7).

In the parable, a shepherd had one hundred sheep, and one wandered off. He left the ninety-nine sheep, and went to find the one. The shepherd probably counted the sheep at intervals to make sure he had them all because sheep wander off to find greener grass or just because they do not know any better.

We know that the shepherd had a deep concern for the lost sheep, but how did the lost sheep feel about being lost? The sheep probably felt like most of us when we stray away from Jesus. At first, we think we know where we are going. Then, we realize that we cannot find our way back. We grow confused and fearful and regret that we strayed from our shepherd. We wish that we had never left in the first place. We wonder if anyone will find us and bring us back to safety. No matter how far we have strayed and how lost we are in the wilderness of life, help is on the way!

Like the shepherd in the parable, Jesus is concerned about each of us. The lost sheep shows us that we can be under the leadership of Jesus, the

Good Shepherd, and still get lost in our sins. This can be a scary place just like being lost in a jungle. Jesus is constantly searching for sinners — people whom others have forgotten and written off. Jesus is looking for all of us. Jesus' grace is so abundant and his love is so deep for us, that regardless of how much we continue to get lost, he continues to make himself available to us. He promised never to leave us alone.

Help is on the way!

Grace reveals to us that we are better, and we can get better in spite of our sinfulness.

I'm Getting Better

Teachers frequently assess students' progress, first to see what they already know and then to measure their increased knowledge. Our lives are like classroom environments. Sometimes, we sit in a classroom listening to a lecture. At other times, we are in laboratories putting what we have heard in the classroom into practice. Regardless of the setting, God is teaching us and giving us the tools to get better. None of us are perfect. No matter how much we say we love God, we always have room for improvement

In Psalm 51, we witness a remorseful David. Although he was a man after God's own heart, he still had lessons to learn. David wrote this Psalm in response to his decision to use his power as king to act on his sexual impulses. He had sex with Bathsheba and killed her husband, Uriah, to cover up the affair and the resulting pregnancy. David had much to learn. David teaches us about the availability and power of God's grace. His confession and plea for forgiveness in our Scripture show us that regardless of how badly we have messed up that we can take steps to get better. If we go through life believing we can get better, we will see ourselves growing and improving.

All of us were born with a sin problem—Indeed, I was born guilty, a sinner when my mother conceived me (Psalm 51:5). Our innate sinfulness poses a hindrance to us to believe that we can get better. This is why we need God's grace. The grace of God helps us to overcome this spiritual birth defect. Grace gives us understanding, direction, and the desire to act counter to our proclivity to sin. Grace reveals to us that we are better, and we can get better in spite of our sinfulness.

God is always assessing our progress. If God sees that we are not where we should be, God will put circumstances in our life so that we can increase our faith and deepen our worship and praise. God wants us to get better. This is God's grace at work. Be encouraged. Testify—I'm getting better.

*When we begin to value who we are and trust in the Lord,
we will wait on the Lord.*

Jesus Is Worth the Wait

A prevalent theme in Scripture is waiting. Waiting is one of the most difficult exercises and lessons that we learn as Christians.

Peter's writings reveal this theological truth: "But do not ignore this one fact, beloved, that with the Lord one day is like a thousand years, and a thousand years are like one day" (2 Peter 3:8). God's time is not our time. Peter's epistle sought to encourage people who began to question whether Jesus Christ would return. They began to lose hope and to doubt as they waited.

Waiting is a human struggle because our flesh makes us believe that God operates on our schedule. We forget that God's delay is not God's denial. As we wait on the manifestation of God's promises, we grow impatient because of their importance in our lives. Rather than waiting for Jesus to bless us, we try to bless ourselves. We start putting things in motion without any direction from Jesus Christ. Years ago, I shopped at a computer auction, and I asked God for a new computer for $500. As the auction progressed, I decided to grab the next deal at $675 because I was afraid that the prices would increase even more. On my way out, I met a woman who had bought a computer with the software, and she shared she had paid $500. This is what happens when we fail to wait.

God's understanding of time is infinite. God is seldom early, but he is never late. Because we lack understanding of the theological time zone, we act outside of God's will to fulfill God's promise to us. Many of us are in unhealthy relationships, dead-end jobs and financial debt because we did not have the patience and the faith to wait on the Lord. Like me with my hasty computer purchase, we convince ourselves that these decisions are God's will, but then we later find out that haste makes waste. God often saves the best for last. We need to wait.

Grace gives us the power to wait. Grace will let us know that the things that we try to put in motion and that the devil has put before us are worthless compared to what God has in store for us. Sometimes, we do not believe Jesus is worth the wait because we do not believe we are worth the wait. However, we are worth everything God has in store for us.

When we begin to value who we are and trust in the Lord, we will wait on the Lord. Be encouraged. For, one day is like a thousand years, and a thousand years are like one day on his watch.

*The climb is doing God's will, moving toward divine destiny
and deciding daily to follow Jesus.*

Life is a Climb

Life is like climbing a mountain. Every step counts, we must hang on with dear life, and we get tired as we strive to go to the top. Instead of a safety harness around our waist, we are totally dependent on God if we slip, and we often do. Despite the difficulties, we must continue to climb.

Jesus, Peter, James and John climbed the Mountain of Transfiguration. (Matthew 17:1-9). This journey was an opportunity for the disciples to see Jesus transfigured, revealed in all of his glory. Peter, James and John had no idea what would transpire at the end of the climb. But they still made the climb.

Life is a climb. The climb is doing God's will, moving toward divine destiny and deciding daily to follow Jesus. As we climb, we may not know exactly what will happen when we reach the top, but if we are climbing the mountain with Jesus, we will find out that the sore hands, legs, and feet were worth the climb. We cannot appreciate reaching the top unless we experience the challenges and struggles getting there. We mature and grow while we climb. As we make our way up, God is preparing us to witness his glory.

Too many people lose ground because they believe that the climb is not even worth it. They question the purpose of the climb. That is why we see many people throwing their lives away, keeping them on a downward spiral rather than an upward climb. The climb is worth it, and we are worth the climb. After seeing Jesus, Moses and Elijah transfigure, Peter desired to build them tabernacles. He thought they would remain on the top, but he was confused. There are always other climbs, other lessons to learn and other tests to complete. In life, we are constantly climbing.

Every climb moves us closer to Jesus. When our faith starts to shake, our arms and legs may give out. In these moments, Jesus gives us the strength to climb. Life is not a crystal stair consisting of elevators and escalators; it is a climb.

Life is short— like a vapor. This is why we have to get the most out of it and make sure that God is the center of our life

Life Is Too Short

We have all heard the statement, "Life is too short." It is really true. As I see how quickly my children have grown, I realize life is too short. Even if we live to be 1,000, life does not last that long compared to eternity.

Because life is so short, we must seize every moment, make the best of it and get the most from it. We need not live with regrets. We should take advantage of each new day. James' epistle gives us this insight on life. "Come now, you who say, 'Today or tomorrow we will go to such and such a town and spend a year there, doing business and making money.' Yet you do not even know what tomorrow will bring. What is your life? For you are a mist that appears for a little while and then vanishes" (James 4:13-14).

Life is short— like a vapor. This is why we have to get the most out of it and make sure that God is the center of our life. We cannot limit what we do with our lives. To make the most of it, we must invest in it. Whether it is money, time, work, love or endurance, we have to put something into it to get something out of it. Then, regardless of how short our life is, we can know we made the most of it. When we go through this life with faith and hope in God, we are guaranteed to live eternally in heaven.

Without embracing the love of Jesus that follows us all the days of our lives, we could not walk through sickness, hurt and pain. Some people think their life is over when a relationship ends, they lose a job or they receive news of a terminal illness. However, when we experience these deep hurts, life is just beginning. If we allow these circumstances to strengthen us, we can experience a new and better life that witnesses to God's goodness and love.

Certainly, life can get rough. Look at the state of our nation – hatred and disunity. Look at the state of our world – wars, killings and fear. Look at our personal lives – hurt, pain, disappointment and struggle. However, as long as we breathe, we have hope. We have another chance. We can take another step toward improving our lives. We can live out this hope if we keep the faith. At the end of the journey, we will declare that we made it with God on our side.

Be encouraged. Life is too short.

There are survivors who can attest to how God's grace and love enabled them to live through guilt, shame, hurt and other life-threatening disappointments.

Live Through It!

Perhaps you have heard the saying, "Whatever doesn't kill you makes you stronger." The prophet Habakkuk closed his lamentation to God during a time of desolation in Israel's history with these words, "Though the fig tree does not bud and there are no grapes on the vines, though the olive crop fails and the fields produce no food, though there are no sheep in the pen and no cattle in the stalls, yet I will rejoice in the Lord, I will be joyful in God my Savior" (Habakkuk 3:17-18). Like Habakkuk in the early chapters, we complain and lament over our suffering, and sometimes what we go through is so difficult and seemingly unbearable, we feel like surely we will die. The truth is we will live through it. We will live, and not die.

We all experience the unproductive fig tree and vines and the dying cattle in our lives. Yes, the loss of a love one can make us feel as if we cannot go on; sadness and depression can kill just like a smoking gun. Teenagers take their lives because people bully them and make them feel beaten down and worthless. We need to encourage one another through tough times so we can keep on living. Habakkuk reminds us that we can live through all of this if we find encouragement in God's love.

Some people are alive, but they are not living through their circumstances. They are discouraged, unhappy, angry, and experiencing other emotions that keep them from experiencing joy. The truth is no matter how bad the situation is, we can get through it with prayer and praise. There are survivors who can attest to how God's grace and love enabled them to live through guilt, shame, hurt and other life-threatening disappointments.

Let us be encouraged as we go through life's twists and turns. We can never give up on ourselves. We can live through it.

When fear is at work, faith cannot act.

Peter Decided to Follow Jesus

Peter decided to follow Jesus. At Lake Gennesaret, a crowd had gathered around Jesus to hear the Word of God. Through this huge crowd, Jesus spotted Peter's boat on the lake. Jesus got into Peter's boat and continued preaching to the crowd while Peter and his fellow fishermen cleaned their nets. He stopped in the middle of his sermon, asked Peter to push the boat out into the deep and cast his net. Peter, an experienced fisherman, knew this instruction was ridiculous, especially since he had fished in the deep all night and caught no fish. Peter, nevertheless, obeyed Jesus. It paid off because he caught so many fish that the boat began to sink. Without hesitancy, Peter went from career to calling – fishing for souls. (Luke 5:11). He decided to follow Jesus.

Many of us are not like Peter, who immediately quit what he was doing to follow Jesus. Most of us would have contemplated a way to fit Jesus' calling into our schedules, figured a way out of it or simply ignored it. To respond like Peter requires us to operate in faith. When fear is at work, faith cannot act. Often, what we are doing may seem like a sure and safe thing and the goals for which we are striving are within our reach and control, but Jesus wants to do more in our lives. Peter's experience reveals that if we are willing to obey Jesus, he can provide us with an overflow of blessings and give us the grace to follow him.

Peter had a choice to live out his life as a career fisherman, or to lose his life and gain everything in following Jesus. Jesus may call when we are preoccupied with our own visions and goals: busy with school, work, children, marriage and other responsibilities. Regardless of when, where, and how Jesus invites us to follow him, we must be willing to drop everything and accept his invitation. We must rely on his unfailing record to empower and care for us as we live for him and through him.

Jesus is tenderly calling today. Answer.

The mind, body and spirit must be in balance to maintain healthy lifestyles in all aspects of our being.

Physically Fit for Spiritual Fitness

Staying physically fit is difficult because it requires time, energy, work and sacrifice. Unfortunately, many people do not think they need to engage in an exercise routine or practice good eating habits to maintain a healthy and physically fit body able to fulfill God's service in ministry. The importance of following an exercise regime and a healthy diet is not to achieve six-pack abs or a perfect figure. We practice these good habits to stay healthy, live longer and maintain a balanced spiritual life.

Studies have shown that exercise increases energy levels, releases stress and lowers the potential for heart attack, stroke and high blood pressure. When we care for our physical bodies, we tell God that we appreciate the body God has given us, affirm our love for God and ourselves and exercise good stewardship. Our bodies are the temple of the Holy Ghost: "Do you not know that you are God's temple and that God's Spirit dwells in you? For God's temple is holy, and you are that temple" (1 Corinthians 3:16-17).

We should care for the temple through spiritual fitness and physical exercise. Exercise for the body and spirit are directly related. When we take care of the physical body by eating right and exercising the body, we are also taking care of the spirit. As we pray for spiritual strength and cleansing, we must recognize our power to strengthen and cleanse our physical bodies. How many of us can eat just one potato chip, slice of pizza, cookie, or piece of fried chicken? It is hard to resist. For many of us going to the gym is like going to church, once we get started, we go regularly, but if we miss a day, we start to slack off completely. It's not easy taking care of our temple. We need God's grace to give us discipline to eat right and exercise.

Many people are in shape physically, but out of shape spiritually. They are perfectly fit. They eat clean. They practically live in the gym, but they have no relationship with God. The physical body will eventually break down just like a car due to age and other biological realities. This is why we must be spiritually fit. We must eat clean spiritually and live a life after God, which keeps us in good shape when we experience life's challenges.

The mind, body and spirit must be in balance to maintain healthy lifestyles in all aspects of our being. When we treat our bodies like temples of the Holy Spirit, we do everything in moderation and to the glory of God. Then, we will become physically fit for spiritual fitness.

Our walls go through struggles, storms and other tragedies that tear them down.

Rebuild Me

Survivors of domestic violence, cancer or even plane crashes will say that getting through the struggle requires restoration and recovery. Going through illness, violence or any near-death experience is only part of being a survivor. The tough part is recovering from the hurt, fear and fatigue, which are natural consequences of suffering.

This is exactly what the Israelites who remained in Jerusalem were experiencing. The walls of their community were torn down. They needed recovery and rebuilding. Although the people of Israel had escaped the worst part of the situation, they still felt as if they had been destroyed. The walls of Jerusalem were torn down. They were walking around in the middle of destruction and the aftermath of war and chaos.

Nehemiah, away from his people, had inquired about how everyone was doing in Jerusalem. To his dismay, he learned that the walls of Jerusalem were destroyed and the people who made it out of captivity were struggling: "The survivors there in the province who escaped captivity are in great trouble and shame; the wall of Jerusalem is broken down, and its gates have been destroyed by fire" (Nehemiah 1:3b).

When Nehemiah heard about the state of Jerusalem, he sought permission to return to his hometown to rebuild the walls so the people, the remaining survivors, could be restored. The restoration of Jerusalem meant the recovery of their relationship with God, their dignity and their humanity. Nehemiah and a team of men joined together to rebuild the walls of Jerusalem.

When Nehemiah began repairing the walls, some people tried to discourage him and his helpers. They implemented tactics to convince Nehemiah that the walls could not be rebuilt. They even threatened his life and the lives of the workers. But Nehemiah refused to quit until the work had been completed.

Our walls go through struggles, storms and other tragedies that tear them down. However, God's grace can rebuild us. Like James Olson rebuilt Steve Austin, the Six Million Dollar Man, God can and will do the same for us. When God remakes us and repairs and restores our situations, we no longer have the same fears or make the same choices. We are stronger, wiser and better. As we go through challenges in life, people may tear us down, but we have the blessed assurance of knowing we are survivors, and God will rebuild us, one brick at a time. Rebuild me!

When we do our homework, we allow the Word to speak to us and have a personal witness to Scripture and its power in our lives.

Rightly Proclaiming the Word of Truth

Paul advises his protégé, Timothy, as he embarks upon his call, "Do your best to present yourself to God as one approved by him, a worker who has no need to be ashamed, rightly proclaiming the word of truth" (2 Timothy 2:15). Paul gives Timothy this instruction because he understands that the more a person studies, the more knowledgeable of and comfortable the individual is with the material.

When we engage in God-talk with others, we may feel ashamed to rightly proclaim the word of truth. We may lack confidence in talking about God and other theological matters because we have not done our homework. Then we may question our ability to understand and talk about God's Word. We start to think that others have superior knowledge in these areas, but that's not it; our knowledge is just as sharp. We simply may not have done our homework.

When I was in one of my theology classes at Vanderbilt, everyone seemed so engaged in the material. They sounded like experts, answering questions, and speaking intellectually on difficult topics. I remained silent. Because I had not read the assignment, I had to depend on the rightness of other's opinions. I could not make a contribution of my own. Had I done my homework and prepared, I could have made a contribution and sounded as intelligent as my colleagues.

We need to study for ourselves, to make the Word real and relevant for us. When we do our homework, we allow the Word to speak to us and have a personal witness to Scripture and its power in our lives. Although we may not understand everything we read, studying the Word puts us in God's very presence. The more we study the Word, the more we grow in grace. As we grow in the love of God, God will reveal the meaning of Scripture to us so that we can rightly proclaim the Word of truth.

We know we are ready to surrender to God when the Holy Spirit speaks to us to go, and we respond without mumbling, talking back and making excuses—send me!

Send Me!

We often restrict ministry to those whom God has called to preach. The truth is God calls all of us to be ministers to someone or at some place. Ministry extends beyond preaching and pastoring a church. God prepares us for our individual callings, and we must be ready to answer and prepared to go where he tells us to go. Send me.

Isaiah, a prophet, answered his call in the year King Uzziah died. He had a vision of God in which an angel touched his lips with a live piece of coal to deal with his thoughts of uncleanness and worthiness. God is so faithful to us, God will call us even when we have unclean lips. The prophet wrote, "Then I heard the voice of the Lord saying, 'Whom shall I send, and who will go for us?' And I said, 'Here am I; send me!'"(Isaiah 6:8). Our objective – after knowing there is life after death and that there is Resurrection on the other side of our pain and sin – should be a resounding agreement to do God's work.

Isaiah was ready to go without hesitation. Before God sends us, God prepares us. We may not like the way God prepares us to do his work because sometimes it is painful. In Isaiah's case, God prepared him with a piece of live coal to his lips to cleanse him of his sinfulness.

We have had some live coal experiences in which God was preparing us for our calling. If we give thought to the challenges, disappointments and rejections we have faced in our lives, we would realize how God readied us for his divine work. We cannot volunteer to go if we have not been prepared, pruned, humbled and matured. God is patient, and he will keep checking in with us to make sure we are ready.

We know we are ready to surrender to God when the Holy Spirit speaks to us to go, and we respond without mumbling, talking back and making excuses—send me! God does not need to tell us where to go or beg us to go; we know the places that need hope and restoration. We should go forth with a willing and obedient spirit. Send me to the juvenile justice center to help hopeless youth. Send me to the corners in blighted neighborhoods where women are abused. Send me to where children are exploited. Send me to those who cry out for justice and need to be heard. Send me; I'll go!

We have to be honest with ourselves as to whether we really want to leave our mats.

Stand, Take Up Your Mat and Walk

We have all been in situations where we may feel like healing and deliverance are impossible. The healing of the man at the pool of Bethesda lets us know that regardless of what is happening around us, he is available to heal us in spite of ourselves. At Bethesda, "lay many invalids – blind, lame, and paralyzed." Jesus noticed a paralytic man on his mat. He had been sick for thirty-eight years. When Jesus asked the man whether he wanted to be made well, he responded, "Sir, I have no one to put me into the pool when the water is stirred up; and while I am making my way, someone else steps down ahead of me." Jesus said, "Stand up, take your mat and walk" (John 5:1-8). Perhaps, if we were in the man's shoes, most of us would have given Jesus an emphatic, "Yes." The man, however, focused on why he could not walk, instead of believing he could.

The paralytic man had many problems in addition to his mat. He did not know Jesus, depended on other people to bless him, did not know how to be healed, procrastinated and focused more on his sickness than on being made well. Other sick people stepped in front of him when the pool stirred. They cut line because they thought that if he went in front of them, he would get healed and they wouldn't. Instead of lifting one another up and making each other well, they step in front of and all over each other.

We may not be confined like the man at the pool, but we still find ourselves on mats. These are mats of sin, procrastination, selfishness, infidelity, addiction, low self-esteem, depression and other mats that prevent us from standing on God's promises and walking into our divine destinies.

We have to be honest with ourselves as to whether we really want to leave our mats. Jesus is asking us whether we want to be healed. Many of us are guilty like the paralytic in our story who focused more on his problem than the solution. It is time for us to take up our mats.

When people are unable to help us, Jesus will be there. He is able to do more than put us in a pool. He can speak deliverance, healing, and hope into our situations. Jesus loves us so much he gives us what we need, even though we do not deserve it. Stand, take up your mat and walk!

*We must look to what lies ahead and strive for our goals, even
if it requires us to strain, press and struggle.*

Strive for Your Goals

We make commitments to ourselves to exercise, stop smoking, lose weight, read the Bible daily and pray more. Although we commit to improve our lives, we have trouble with following through. Often, when we try to do right or change for the better, we encounter obstacles that deter us from the goal and prevent its fulfillment. When these situations arise, we may become discouraged and give up on pursuing the goal. We cannot quit; we must strive for our goals.

Paul wrote, "Beloved, I do not consider that I have made it my own; but this one thing I do: forgetting what lies behind and straining forward to what lies ahead, I press on toward the goal for the prize of the heavenly call of God in Christ Jesus" (Philippians 3:13-14).

These brief words of Scripture reveal that in our lives, we will meet discouragement. It appears in the form of negative thinking, environments and people. Many of us cannot move forward because we keep looking back. We must not let the past to control our future and our ability to keep reaching and striving for the prize of the heavenly call of God in Christ Jesus. We must look to what lies ahead and strive for our goals, even if it requires us to strain, press and struggle.

In God's Word, we find a wealth of promises that keep hope burning in our hearts. Paul's wisdom encompasses a promise upon which we can rest assured that even in the midst of our weaknesses, in those periods of our lives when we feel like giving up, God gives us the strength to overcome and rise above our circumstances. God is the prize at the end of the race.

No matter how hard it gets, we can reach our goals. The Tennessee Titans and the Buffalo Bills were in the last few seconds of a final play-off game to determine which team would play in the Super Bowl. Many thought the game was over until Kevin Dyson ran 75 yards down the left sideline with a lateral pass on a kickoff with three seconds remaining in the game. Dyson ran the ball into the goal line and scored a winning touchdown in seconds.

Don't you know that God sees you in your last few seconds, the seconds that you need for your breakthrough, your touchdown? God will position everything and bring you over the goal line.

Be encouraged! Strive for your goals.

Barriers such as race, gender, class, and how a person smells should not impede access to God's grace. God cares about each of us and makes grace and love available to us.

Through the Roof

While living in Atlanta, I did not have a car. I walked a mile to church from the bus stop downtown. On my way to a Sunrise service, a homeless man spoke to me. He had come from under a bridge. Initially, I felt unsafe and wanted to keep walking. But my spirit responded to this man with a smile and an invitation to church. To my surprise, he indicated he wanted to go and said with disappointment, "But the liquor." He reeked with alcohol. Nevertheless, I encouraged the man to accompany me. "Well, you are sick," I told him. "The church is a hospital for sinners."

The man walked to church with me. The church was filled to capacity. We found two cramped seats in the back of the church. As we listened to the service, a woman passed a peppermint to the man. At that moment, I said to myself: "Every one of us in this place has some stink on us." The man needed more than a peppermint. He needed to be brought from guilt to grace. He needed prayer, support and encouragement.

The church often acts like the world when it comes to people who are struggling and needing the warmth and love of Jesus Christ. In Mark 2, we witness friends tearing off the roof of a house to lower their paralytic friend for an opportunity for Jesus to heal him. "And when they could not bring him to Jesus because of the crowd, they removed the roof above him; and after having dug through it, they let down the mat upon which the paralytic lay" (Mark 2:4). The crowd often puts challenges, barriers and other stumbling blocks in the way of those who really need to experience the healing touch of Jesus Christ in a church setting. Given the condition of this man, paralyzed and on a mat, it would seem the crowd would have made room for him to come through the door. Instead, they blocked the way and gave him a peppermint.

God is available to all of us. Barriers such as race, gender, class, and how a person smells should not impede access to God's grace. God cares about each of us and makes grace and love available to us. No matter what obstacles try to stop us from getting to God, he provides good friends, a law student walking down the streets of Atlanta, or someone unexpected inviting us to church to make sure that we can experience forgiveness and all other benefits from being in the presence of Jesus Christ, even if it means tearing off the roof.

What enabled this man to experience forgiveness and the ability to walk again was determination and faith. His friends did not give up. When we go through the roof for Jesus, we will leave out the front door with a testimony of healing and forgiveness.

We must realize that each struggle brings us closer to our divine destiny.

Too Close

The hardest part of any journey is when it is almost over. It seems when we are on the verge of a breakthrough after a long wait or hard struggle, we are faced with the decision to finish or go back to "start." The road can become so difficult that we are tempted to give up.

Far from Egypt and close to the Promised Land, the Israelites were tempted to go back to Egypt. On their journey to the Promised Land, the Israelites spent most of the journey wandering in the wilderness. (Numbers 33:1-50). They wandered from Rameses in Egypt to the plains of Moab near Jericho. A three-week trip turned into a 40-year journey. They had to go through the wilderness. As they got closer to their destination, they wanted to return to Egypt because things seemed unbearable in the wilderness. They were on the edge of their blessing and did not know it.

Like the Israelites, we are on the brink of our Promised Land. Often what separates us from where we are and where God has destined us to be is where we are spiritually. When we are in the middle of the road, in the wilderness, we must remember that God is preparing us for the promise. Each setback or hurdle we face along the way is an opportunity for God to prepare us for the great and wonderful thing or place in store for us. Rather than allowing these obstacles to equip us and grow our faith, we feel as though they are signs that the promise is not true and there is no purpose or plan in store. Therefore, we want to go back to Egypt. Many do give up and return to Egypt, only to realize they were just a prayer away from their destination.

We must realize that each struggle brings us closer to our divine destiny. Struggle often causes delay and may even require more deliverance. Just because God took us out of Egypt does not mean that we do not have some Egypt left in us. God wants us to go to the Promised Land free of Egypt. For this reason, God takes us the long way, the wilderness, to get to his promises, but rest assured; we will get there. The wilderness tries our faith, but it makes us better. When we are on the last leg of our journey, the enemy will try to make us go backward and give us a hard time, but we must keep moving forward to see what the end will be because we are too close.

There is no need to waste our time wishing bad on someone when we can use our time doing something that brings us joy and God the glory. Turn the other cheek.

Turn the Other Cheek

Communities and families struggle with hate, anger and conflict. What the world needs now is to love like Jesus. Jesus taught us how to love and to end hatred, anger and conflict. "You have heard that it was said, 'An eye for an eye and a tooth for a tooth.' But I say to you, do not resist an evildoer. But if anyone strikes you on the right cheek, turn the other also" (Matthew 5:38-39). Turn the other cheek.

Often when someone hurts us, our human instinct is to hurt them back. Too many of us spend our lives trying to take an eye for an eye and a tooth for a tooth, or hoping someone else will do it for us. If we cannot take the eye or tooth as payment for what someone did to us, we harbor and nurture the pain. We need to turn the other cheek. Because someone hits us or says something ugly to us, it does not mean that we have to respond or have a right to respond in the same way. Turning the other cheek or taking the high road takes love – the love Jesus exemplified through his life, death and Resurrection. It is no longer an eye for an eye and a tooth for a tooth; it is turn the other cheek. Love. Forgive. There is no need to waste our time wishing bad on someone when we can use our time doing something that brings us joy and God the glory. Turn the other cheek.

When we turn the other cheek, we gain authority over our hurt and our ability to heal. We no longer let these negative emotions have control over our lives. When a person forgives, anger and hate disappear. When we truly love the people who did us wrong, the problems they caused are no longer ours; they belong to them.

We could end some of the ills in this world, if we would love one another as Jesus Christ loves each of us. If we turned the other cheek, the prison population would decrease, families would be healed and the world would be at peace. Rather than going through the trouble of snatching out a person's eye or tooth, turn the other cheek.

*We have nothing to fear. God has not given us a spirit of fear,
but of power, love and a sound mind. These are the strengths
we need to operate in faith and against fear.*

What Do You Have to Fear?

Franklin D. Roosevelt said, "The only thing we have to fear is fear itself." He meant that fear – not the thing, situation or person we may fear – is our real enemy.

"For God did not give us a spirit of cowardice, but rather a spirit of power and of love and of self-discipline" (2 Timothy 1:7). Fear is more than an emotion; it is a spirit. It can prevent us from experiencing all that God has for us and can lead to unnecessary feelings of depression, anxiety and paranoia. We must not succumb to the spirit of fear. It does not come from God. The spirit of fear originates in our flesh. The devil does a great job of maximizing our fears, spooks us out of many blessings and opportunities and convinces us to believe things that are not really true about ourselves or situations. Fear is dangerous.

We have nothing to fear. God has not given us a spirit of fear, but of power, love and a sound mind. These are the strengths we need to operate in faith and against fear. All of us have some type of phobia. Some of us are scared of water, heights, being in closed places and the dark. These are common phobias. Some people even fear being blessed, being great, being healed and simply being what God has called them to be. Everyone has a different fear, but the spirit of fear operates in the same way with each of us, but we do not have to cooperate with it.

If we have phobias and cooperate with them, we will never get the most out of life. We will continue to make decisions based on fear. We will permit fear to keep us from entering healthy and whole relationships, keep us from progressing professionally, keep us from living holy lives, and keep us from doing the things God calls us to do.

Yes, we will have some fears, some hesitations in this life, but we must try to rise above them with the wisdom of FDR – The only thing we have to fear is fear itself. When we realize how wonderful our God is and how much God loves us, we will experience the power, love and sound mind God gave us.

What do you have to fear?

We must confess the name of Jesus, believe in his Resurrection and allow his grace to transform us, making us spiritual beings who serve God and do God's will.

What Must I do to Be Saved?

Plenty of books tell us how to be better salespeople, be happy every day, make more money and be a leader. These resources are usually written by people who are successful. They are the experts.

The world needs to hear from the experts on the pivotal question, "What must I do to be saved?" A curious Nicodemus sought the answer to this question from Jesus. (John 3:1-10) He wanted to know more about Jesus.

Although many people want to know the answer to the question—what must I do to be saved—they are unwilling to consult with the experts. However, the Nicodemus types want to know. They satisfy their curiosity with people who carry and read their Bibles, Sunday school teachers, pastors, parents and deacons who are honest about their faith and practice what they preach. For me, Dorothy Talbert and Beatrice Peterkin taught me the Word of God and equipped me to teach others as a teenager through Bible cards, Sunday school and their personal witness.

Nicodemus does not ask Jesus a question; he makes a statement: "Rabbi, we know that you are a teacher who has come from God; for no one can do these signs that you do apart from the presence of God" (John 3:2b). Jesus explains to Nicodemus, "Very truly, I tell you, no one can see the kingdom of God without being born from above... No one can enter the kingdom of God without being born of water and Spirit" (John 3:3-5). We as Christians must be prepared for the Nicodemus types who want to know about Jesus!

When we witness people struggling with addiction, sinful living, worry and depression, they are crying, "What must I do to be saved?" Like Jesus revealed to Nicodemus, we must be born again to experience God's grace and mercy. We must confess the name of Jesus, believe in his Resurrection and allow his grace to transform us, making us spiritual beings who serve God and do God's will.

Only the experts possess the answer to "What must I do to be saved?" The experts are not necessarily noted theologians and people who have gone to divinity school or who have a lengthy resume. We who have been born of the water and of the spirit are the experts.

We can testify that Jesus is the answer to salvation and to eternal life.

We must believe in ourselves and know that God finds worth in what we have, who we are and how we are made. Even if we make mistakes, God still finds us worthy.

You Are Worth Saving

Insurance adjusters are often called out to evaluate the damage of automobiles after a car accident. They essentially determine the value of the car and compare it to the amount of damage assessed on the vehicle. Some accidents damage vehicles so badly that they are not worth the money or the time to fix. This cost analysis is determining whether the vehicle is worth saving. If the vehicle is totaled, then its end is a junk yard, split into many pieces, and compressed into a box of metal.

Fortunately, God believes all of us are worth saving regardless of how badly we are damaged. The cost of repairing and rescuing are never greater than our worth. David recalls the number of times God saved Israel and rescued the people from their enemies. David writes, "Blessed be the Lord, who has not given us as prey to their teeth. We have escaped like a bird from the snare of the fowlers; the snare is broken, and we have escaped" (Psalm 124:6-7).

Most of us have been, are or will be in the position of the Israelites, under attack and in need of saving. We are all in need of being rescued from sin, and we are all worth being rescued. God wants to save us. God values us and makes a way for us to escape crazy situations. How many times today did we find ourselves regretting something we said or did? God came along, cut the ropes and freed us to do his will and live out our destinies. God decided that we are worth saving! God never gives up on us. We will never end up in a junk yard or become prey to our enemies.

I entered a chili contest at my children's elementary school. The red ribbon was between my crock-pot and the one next to mine. Although the official told me that my chili had won for my category, the chili pots on both sides of mine were empty and mine remained full. No one was eating my chili. How could my chili be the winning chili and no one was eating it? Many of us have not walked into our destinies because we are too concerned with who is not eating our chili.

We let others determine our worth rather than relying on God's approval. If God likes our chili, it does not matter who else likes it. God thinks it is a winner. We must believe in ourselves and know that God finds worth in what we have, who we are and how we are made. Even if we make mistakes, God still finds us worthy. God will break the snare and rescue us from the fowler. In God's eyes, we are worth saving.

We learn from Hannah that if we sincerely turn over our hurt to God, he will lift our burdens and put a smile on our face.

You Look Better When You Smile

One of the kindest gestures to give someone is a smile. Some of us only smile in good times, when posing for a picture or while someone is tickling our feet or tummy. These things can make us smile, but we also must learn to smile when we face challenges and adversities because we look better when we smile. The second chapter of I Samuel begins with a very joyous mother, Hannah, who in the previous chapter had struggled with depression because she could not have a baby.

The husband's other wife, who could have children made fun of Hannah's barrenness. Hannah could not smile, even when her husband tried to make her smile by showing love and support. After praying over her situation, the man of God, Elijah, who overheard Hannah's prayers assured her that she would give birth to a son. In due time, she gave birth to Samuel. This event put a smile on her face. "Hannah prayed with thanksgiving, 'My heart exults in the Lord; my strength is exalted in my God. My mouth derides my enemies, because I rejoice in my victory'" (1 Samuel 2:1).

We have all been in Hannah's shoes. We find it difficult to smile at our situations and struggles. We deal with people or circumstances that try to convince us that we have no reason to smile. We learn from Hannah that if we sincerely turn over our hurt to God, he will lift our burdens and put a smile on our face. We look and feel better when we choose to smile through life's challenges and defeats.

God may have closed Hannah's womb, but he still was smiling down on her. God's presence, power and love put a smile on Hannah's face.

When we see God's smile, we can exchange our sad face for a smiley face. Surely, God has smiled on us and set us free.

We can smile through tears, hurt and discouragement. We can even smile at our enemies. Our smiles will lift us up. When we smile, we radiate God's grace. We declare that our circumstances are not greater than the joy God has placed inside us, which makes us smile. Things can have an effect on us, but nothing means as much as our smile.

Keep smiling. You look better.

Be Assured

Be Assured

Bounce back · 73
Dry Bones Can Live · 75
Every Step · 77
God Does Not Forget Us · 79
God Gives Us Victory · 81
God Is for Us · 83
God Is Up to Something · 85
God Supplies All of Our Needs · · · · · · · · · · · · · · · · · 87
God Will Wipe Away Every Tear · · · · · · · · · · · · · · · 89
God's Grace Is Sufficient · 91
God's Love · 93
Got Milk? · 95
Help My Unbelief · 97
How to Build a House · 99
I Got This! · 101
Jesus Saw the Best in Me · 103
Like Job · 105
Lost and Found · 107
My Cup is Running Over · 109
Nothing Just Happens · 111
Our Stripes Can Heal · 113
Put God first · 115
Robin, It's Going to Be All Right · · · · · · · · · · · · · · · 117
Still I Rise · 119
The Best Is Yet to Come · 121
The Palm Tree · 123
There is a Bright Side Somewhere · · · · · · · · · · · · · · 125
Things Are Turning Around! · · · · · · · · · · · · · · · · · · 127
Things Will Work Out · 129
You Are Anointed · 131
You Can Survive a Snakebite · · · · · · · · · · · · · · · · · · 133
You Have Beautiful Feet · 135

The purpose of the affliction is to crush us, the perplexities, to drive us crazy, the persecutions, to make us give up on our faith, and the rejections, to destroy us.

Bounce back

Life is filled with let downs, but if we are willing to remain hopeful, we will experience the power of grace that lifts us up, and saves us from destruction. Paul writes, "We are afflicted in every way, but not crushed; perplexed, but not driven to despair; persecuted, but not forsaken; struck down, but not destroyed" (2 Corinthians 4:8-9).

We must remember that our afflictions, perplexities, persecutions and rejections give us a reason to testify about God's power working in our lives. Without the test, we cannot have a testimony. When we are thrown down in this way, God's grace enables us to bounce back.

The purpose of the affliction is to crush us, the perplexities, to drive us crazy, the persecutions, to make us give up on our faith, and the rejections, to destroy us. As Paul reminds us, because of Christ in us, these problems will not overtake us. We can bounce back.

Often, when we experience challenges, we wonder whether we will be able to bounce back. If we were delivered immediately from our problems, we would not see God's glory moving in our situations. We would give the glory to something or someone else. God shows us just in the nick of time that he is in control and enables us to make a comeback. These are the times in which we reflect: If God had not been on our side, where would we be? We knew that neither the lawyer, the doctor, nor the preacher deserved the credit. We could not even give it to ourselves. We owed it all to the saving grace and mercy of Jesus Christ.

How can a person suffering with recurrences of cancer testify that although she is afflicted in every way, she is not crushed? How can a person who has AIDS, but no health insurance to pay for treatment testify about not being driven to despair? How can a single mother stand before the church and talk about not being forsaken by God when she and her children struggle to survive financially? How can a man imprisoned for twenty years for a murder he did not commit talk about being struck down, but not destroyed? The answer is God's grace. Grace will not allow the things that sought to take us out accomplish their purpose. We can bounce back from anything and everything. No matter how hard we get knocked down, we will bounce back. The harder we are thrown, the greater our testimony. Bounce back!

In the midst of the valley of dry bones, we will witness God's hand stretching and pulling the pieces together, from the head bone to the toe bone, and then blowing new life into the bodies.

Dry Bones Can Live

Regret, hopelessness and guilt often haunt us and make us think all is lost. However, all that is lost isn't gone. In Ezekiel 37, God took the prophet Ezekiel into a valley of dry bones. God revealed that the valley of dry bones represented the House of Israel. Because of the people's disobedience toward God, they had become a valley of dry bones. They were in exile, and their spiritual life had dried up. The bones were dry, separated and broken.

While Ezekiel sat in the midst of the dry bones, God and Ezekiel struck up a conversation about whether the dry, brittle bones could live. Ezekiel let the answer rest with God whether the dry bones could live. "Then he said to me, 'Prophesy to these bones, and say to them: O dry bones, hear the word of the Lord. Thus says the Lord God to these bones: I will cause breath to enter you, and you shall live. I will lay sinews on you, and will cause flesh to come upon you, and cover you with skin, and put breath in you, and you shall live; and you shall know that I am the Lord'" (Ezekiel 37:4-6). God did it. The dry bones lived and became a mighty army.

All of us have had personal dry-bones experiences: disappointment, rejection, discouragement, loneliness, hurt, and other types of pain. Our community, in many instances, has become a valley of dry bones. Children are neglected and abused—a valley of dry bones. Racial strife among communities has resulted in violence and deaths—a valley of dry bones. Around the world, including the United States, families are starving to death—a valley of dry bones. People are dying unnecessarily because they cannot afford a doctor—a valley of dry bones. The existence of violence in any form is a valley of dry bones. Like Ezekiel, we can look around our world in which God has placed us and see the very dry bones. God is asking us—whether these bones can live.

Some may determine that the dry bones cannot live because the situation is too broken, brittle and dry for life to return to the bones. God's eternal existence means that there is hope for the dry bones. Dry bones can live!

God declares to us that if we are willing to speak life, deliverance and restoration over the bones, they can live! Things will reconnect. In the midst of the valley of dry bones, we will witness God's hand stretching and pulling the pieces together, from the head bone to the toe bone, and then blowing new life into the bodies. When we are spread across the valley of dry bones, in our own exile situations, we have the power to live again and connect with others to become a mighty army for God. Dry bones can live!

If we are willing to trust God on the journey, he will guide our every step.

Every Step

At fifteen months, I watched my daughter, Elizabeth, struggle to climb stairs. My instinct was to help her, but I knew she needed to learn how to conquer those steps.

Learning to walk in the spiritual is just like learning how to walk in the physical. As we grow in grace, we take baby steps and gradually move into a more mature faith. However, like my toddler daughter learning to climb steps, the journey can turn into a real struggle.

In the book of Isaiah, the prophet brings words of comfort to the discouraged Israelites. He lets them know that their journey has been one filled with challenges valleys, mountains, crooked paths, and rocky roads, but God has been with them every step of the way. Isaiah further assures them of God's promise to make their steps on the journey easier and successful: "Every valley shall be lifted up, and every mountain and hill be made low; the uneven ground shall become level, and the rough places plain. Then the glory of the Lord shall be revealed, and all people shall see it together, for the mouth of the Lord has spoken" (Isaiah 40:4-5).

As we go through life, we will meet situations that seem like mountains that are impossible to climb, and low places where we feel like there is no way out, and travel on ground that seems to wind around very dangerous places, but God is present. If we are willing to trust God on the journey, he will guide our every step.

God watches our every step. Even though we may struggle up the stairs, and wonder why God is not helping us, God is watching to make sure we do not fall. When things get too tough, he clears the way and even creates new ways for us to meet divine destiny.

God does this by sending special people into our lives to encourage us, working miracles in the middle of messed up situations, and giving us strength. When we approach mountains, valleys, and bad road conditions, let us not turn around, but know that God has the authority to make those mountains low, to raise valleys, and to make crooked paths straight. As we grow in grace, we will ask God to leave the mountains, the valleys, and the crooked paths in their same condition and give us the grace to conquer them.

Be assured. No matter how difficult the path, God will make a way for every step we take.

God does not forget us. God still provides brooks and ravens to get us through difficult times. God still specializes in impossible circumstances.

God Does Not Forget Us

I remember leaving work and driving down the street on the way home, when I suddenly realized that I had forgotten my infant daughter at her daycare. The horrible feeling that came over me taught me never once again to forget. Sometimes as we go through life, we feel like God has taken off down the street and forgotten to pick us up, especially in those times when it seems as if everyone else has abandoned us. The prophet Elijah found himself in such a dilemma, but he learned that God does not forget about us. (I Kings 17).

After delivering some bad news about drought in the land, Elijah, upon the direction from the Lord hid himself. An innocent Elijah spent his time on the run, fearful for his life, and faced with the possibility of not being able to eat or drink, because as he had prophesied, there was famine in the land. God provided a discouraged Elijah with a brook and a raven to deal with his thirst and hunger.

God is awesome. In the midst of famine, God remembered Elijah. Events around us do not determine what God will do for us. Regardless of the situation, including famine and hardship, God does not forget us.

As in the days of Elijah, we experience famine – shortages of material things, self-respect, love, and discipline. Famine can turn our faith into fear and discouragement. Any time we experience a drought in our lives, it can make us think God does not care.

Like our biblical story reminds us, there is still hope. God does not forget us. God still provides brooks and ravens to get us through difficult times. God still specializes in impossible circumstances. Elijah, a man of faith, showed how God remembers us even when supplies run out and good turns to bad.

Elijah waited and listened for the voice of God to tell him his next move after the ravens stopped coming and the brook dried up. Elijah knew God had not forsaken him. God led Elijah to a widow, who thought God had forgotten her. Even though she and her son were on the verge of starvation with little food, she stepped out on faith and shared what she had left with the man of God. God remembered Elijah, the poor widow, and her son. God enabled them to survive the famine. Even when the widow's son became deathly ill, God remembered her faith, and enabled Elijah to heal her son. Let us not forget that through every situation, God does not forget us.

Having the victory means overcoming, meeting a challenge, refusing to cooperate with fear, rejoicing with others and deciding to try.

God Gives Us Victory

Many of us grew up watching television game shows. We enjoyed these shows because we were happy to see someone win the prizes. We also felt disappointment when someone did not win.

Losing a game, of course, does not hurt as much as experiencing some of the losses life often dishes out. We have learned on this journey that we cannot win everything. We will have disappointments. We have also faced the harsh reality that life is not Burger King – we cannot have it our way.

One of our biggest struggles is handling situations that do not turn out as we had hoped. Some have faced the disappointment of loving someone who did not love them back, and watching that same person loving on someone else. That hurts. Others have had the challenge of being an athlete, and after much practice, time and effort, still not make the team. Who has not experienced competing for a job and not getting it, applying to a school and not being accepted, or participating in a contest and not winning?

When we lose, we look at ourselves as losers and permit jealousy, unworthiness, pity, shame and guilt to keep us from evaluating our situation so we can do better the next time. For us to move forward on the road to victory, we must interpret our "loss" as a steppingstone toward our ultimate victory.

We misunderstand victory. Victory is not winning a Super Bowl Ring, a Green Jacket or a crystal trophy. Victory is a gift from God through Jesus Christ. "But thanks be to God, who gives us the victory through our Lord

Jesus Christ" (1 Corinthians 15:57). Plenty of people have won things, but they still do not have the victory. Having the victory means overcoming, meeting a challenge, refusing to cooperate with fear, rejoicing with others and deciding to try.

For us to be victorious, we must acknowledge the source of our victory: Jesus Christ! We are victorious, even in our losses, because we have Jesus Christ. Even when it looks as if our circumstances are victorious over us, we can claim the victory. When hurt and disappointment come into our lives, and things just do not go our way, remember that neither people nor things give us the victory, but God gives us the victory through Jesus Christ.

The odds were against us, but God was for us.

God Is for Us

In math, we learn the concept of probability. We are given a shape or numbers to determine the likelihood of certain outcomes. As we progress in math, we may take a statistics class, which requires us to analyze data and determine the likelihood of outcomes. In life, we make similar predictions.

Many of us live below our potential. We live in fear of stepping out on faith to answer our call to destiny because after gathering statistical data, we determine in our minds that the odds are against us. The truth is all of us have had the odds stacked against us. We may be members of a marginalized community, or have come from a single-parent home, or been born out of wedlock, or come from very humble beginnings. We may have gone home to violent situations, or struggled financially, or faced a bad medical report. The odds were against us, but God was for us.

"If God is for us, who is against us?" (Romans 8:31b). No matter the odds, we can overcome them with God's help and power. We cannot give up just because things do not weigh in our favor. The odds do not determine our destiny or whether we will win or lose. God does. God is for us. If we operate in the will of God and in truth, God is on our side, and it does not matter who or what is on the other side.

For the odds to work in our favor, we must believe. At the end of "Avatar," the main character and ally to the native people, Jake, prayed and asked for victory for the native people because he knew the odds were against them. All they had were bows and arrows, horses and flying dragons, but the humans had modern military technology on their side. The odds were against the natives, but they won in the end. Although this is fiction, the reality is that our prayers can turn the odds in our favor. If God is for us, who can be against us? Let us be encouraged even when the odds are against us, because God is for us.

Often, what we think we need is not what is best for us.

God Is Up to Something

Sometimes we find ourselves in crazy, seemingly impossible situations, and we feel as if we are in the Twilight Zone. When we find ourselves in these circumstances, we need to remember that God always is up to something.

God reveals this important truth through the prophet Isaiah. "For my thoughts are not your thoughts, nor are your ways my ways, says the Lord. For as the heavens are higher than the earth, so are my ways higher than your ways and my thoughts than your thoughts" (Isaiah 55:8-9). God is in control. God knows what is best for us.

We may have an idea or a plan on how God is going to answer our prayers, solve a problem or bless us, but that is not necessarily how God sees the situation. This is when our thoughts come in conflict with God's. If God is working out the situation in a certain way, we may think God is not even on the case. Not only is God not acting in the way we expect him to act, God also is taking his time with the issue. During these moments, our faith starts to weaken.

When we find ourselves losing hope, we must remember what God said to the people of Israel through the prophet. God's perception of our situation is much clearer than ours because God sees the bigger picture. We may just be concerned with what we think we need and how our circumstances have an impact on us rather than God's kingdom. Often, what we think we need is not what is best for us. Things would be easier if we could read God's mind.

How many times have we scooted God over to the passenger seat, taking charge of our situations, answering our own prayers, trying to force God's hand and then seeing things eventually fall apart? No matter how long we have to wait on God to make his presence and power known, God is always up to something.

Although we may experience tragedy, death, loss, hurt, rejection, pain and crises that make us question God's activity in our lives; we can never forget that God is up to something. When we face adversity, God is about to reveal more of his ways and thoughts.

As we go through life's challenges and wait for God to do something, we can be encouraged, knowing God is up to something. God's ways and thoughts are greater than we can conceive. God is up to something.

Once we realize God supplies our needs, we can yield to God's will, do his bidding, not let others control us, and give him the glory.

God Supplies All of Our Needs

Plenty of people believe they cannot start their day without a cup of coffee or finish the day without an energy drink. However, we really can have an energized day without a cup of coffee or an energy supplement. Jesus is all we need. Paul reminds us as he did the church at Philippi, "And my God will fully satisfy every need of yours according to his riches in glory in Christ Jesus" (Philippians 4:19). No one but God can supply our needs.

We all know how hard it is to leave a relationship, even when it is unhealthy for us. Too many of us know the difficult journey of grieving and healing from the loss of a love one. Smoking, nail biting, thumb sucking, and being on social media are not easy habits to break. After *Empire* ended its season, my daughter went through withdrawal. We can get attached and depend on anything, including television shows. It is hard to let go of people and even things which have become an intimate part of who we are, whether positive or negative. The truth is we can survive these losses, because God will be there to supply all of our needs.

Sometimes we miss out on the opportunity to fulfill dreams and meet goals because we depend on others to pull us through. Rather than praying about our situation, we beg a human to do what only God can do for us. God supplies our needs. For us to embrace this theological truth, we must teach ourselves the difference between a want and a need. A want is a desire of the flesh. We make harmful decisions because we get caught up in what we want, rather than what is good for us.

We need God's grace to completely rely on God. Grace gives us the power to break loose of people, things, and bad habits that are unhealthy for us and stunt our spiritual growth. Once we realize God supplies our needs, we can yield to God's will, do his bidding, not let others control us, and give him the glory.

In "Spiderman II," Spiderman struggled with the reality that although he had special powers that enabled him to solve problems and rescue people from dangerous situations, he also needed someone to do the same for him. Often our pride gets in the way of our need for God. However, when we run out of supplies for others and can no longer supply our own needs, we must admit our need for God, even if we are the hero. God supplies our needs through various means; all we have to do is trust that he will do it.

God gave us Jesus, who provides for us, strengthens us, forgives us and cares for us. God supplies everything we need.

When this life ends, we will have nothing to cry about—no more diseases, sicknesses, disappointments, rejection, pain, and death. Those things will pass away. Eternal life will begin.

God Will Wipe Away Every Tear

When the judge announced my divorce in open court, I cried uncontrollably, I was in so much pain. Now that years of have passed since that hurt, God wiped away my tears. I don't cry anymore. Crying sends an immediate and strong message of pain and need. It also sends a message of compassion and empathy. I think that is why people cry watching romantic movies or video clips of people helping others.

Contrary to what people think, crying is not gender-specific. Both men and women cry. Some of us may try to hold back the tears, but on the inside we are crying. Another myth is that crying is a sign of weakness. This is not true. It takes strength to show hurt, pain, or suffering. We have all been in a situation that caused us to weep inwardly and outwardly, but the good news is— God will wipe our tears away.

When suffering brings about tears, we can never give up on God. Many of us cry over unhealthy relationships, being let go from a dead-end job or hurt feelings because someone did not agree with us. These situations are not even worth our tears. Death and other losses like my divorce can make someone cry for years. God is there to renew our spirits, bring us joy and restore our hope.

Through our tears, our faith and love for Jesus grows, and we realize there is no reason to cry. God "will wipe away every tear from their eyes. Death will be no more; mourning and crying and pain will be no more, for the first things have passed away" (Revelation 21:4). When this life ends, we will have nothing to cry about—no more diseases, sicknesses, disappointments, rejection, pain, and death. Those things will pass away. Eternal life will begin.

God will wipe away every tear from our eyes, not just in eschatological times, but also now. As we hear the tears of suffering around our world at the hands of terrorists, fatal diseases and all types of abuse, God is drying the eyes of the hurt and broken. As we lean on God's shoulder and shed our tears, his grace and mercy bring comfort, wipe tears from our eyes and assure us that everything will be all right. God will wipe away every tear.

Whatever God does not remove, God gives us the strength to deal with it.

God's Grace Is Sufficient

I remember having splinters in my fingers. They were painful, but having them removed was even more excruciating. When my cousin's long fingernails could not squeeze out the splinter, she would use a heated needle to remove it. Sometimes I thought that keeping the splinter was less painful than having it removed. If a splinter caused me this much agony, just think how much trauma a thorn causes to our flesh. No wonder Paul wanted it out. It hurt!

Paul, the writer of most of the New Testament, struggled with something that weakened him spiritually. (2 Corinthians 12:1-10). In his prayer to have it removed, Paul calls it a thorn. In response to Paul's prayer, the Lord comforts Paul and tells him that his grace is sufficient, and made perfect in weakness. Although we do not know what the thorn is, we know Paul had this painful thorn for a long time in his flesh, and we also know that he did not have the power to remove it so he turned to Jesus. Paul's soliloquy suggests that all of us have a thorn in our flesh, a flaw, a challenge, or a person that keeps nagging at our spirits and weakening our faith. The thorn is our constant reminder of our need for grace, and this is why Paul prays for its removal and why Jesus chooses not to remove it.

The thorn can be so painful sometimes that we are tempted to look to other things and people to deal with our thorn. Neither alcohol, drugs, nor shopping can get rid of the thorn. Neither parents, spouses, intimate partners, nor best friends can detach the thorn. God's grace is sufficient to help us to endure the thorn. Whatever God does not remove, God gives us the strength to deal with it.

The thorn brings forth the power of grace through our weak flesh. Without the thorn, we would not recognize God's power working in our lives. Like us, Paul probably thought the thorn hindered his ministry, but actually it enhanced his calling. Divine power is best displayed against the backdrop of human weakness. As the thorn weakened Paul, grace strengthened him. We need nothing more than God's grace during these times. God's grace is sufficient. God's grace supplies our needs. God's grace keeps us in our right mind. God's grace makes ways out of no way. There is no other solution for the thorn, except God's grace.

Like the thorns on the rose do not stop it from being a beautiful rose, the thorns in our flesh cannot stop us from blossoming into something beautiful and lovely.

Thank God for the thorn. God's grace is sufficient.

We may be murderers, liars, backbiters, adulterers, gossipers or another type of sinner who is in need of repentance, but God keeps loving us.

God's Love

God's love for humanity is amazing. Often, we forget that God loves us so much. As a result, many of us fall into the traps of sin, believe we cannot be forgiven and seek love in the wrong places. We can never forget how much God loves us. As the Psalmist writes about God, "Your faithfulness endures to all generations; you established the earth, and it stands fast" (Psalm 119:90). God is faithful and God's love for us endures; it does not stop. Think about how important it is for us to hear from our spouses, parents, and children the words, "I love you." Knowing God loves us gives us power and brings us comfort. It is a blessed assurance when God shows us how much he loves us. God loves us, and we cannot do anything about it.

No matter how sinful we are or how much we complain, God's love for us endures forever. God's love does not mean that we will always experience good times. It means that as we go through life's challenges, God is present. The devil often likes to convince us that God does not love us, that God is disgusted with us or that God has kicked us to the curb.

We sometimes buy into these thoughts when we sin or we go through loss, sickness and other suffering. We start to walk down this path when we have prayed about a situation, and it seems as if it is going in one of God's ears and out of the other. When we feel God has forgotten and forsaken us, we need to remember that God loves us through every situation. Despite our lack of faith, God remains faithful; he keeps on loving us. We may doubt, forsake and kick God to the curb, but God's love remains steadfast.

God is love. We can count on God's love. We cannot turn God's love away. We may be murderers, liars, backbiters, adulterers, gossipers or another type of sinner who is in need of repentance, but God keeps loving us. Sometimes we may feel like no one loves us, but we must believe that God is with us and will always love us.

This love God has for us is called grace. God demonstrated this love by sending Jesus Christ into the world to save us. It loves us through good and bad. We witness to God's love when we share it with others.

Great is God's faithfulness! God's love keeps going and going.

People who have spiritual milk see their imperfections as opportunities to become perfected.

Got Milk?

Remember the public service ads encouraging us to drink milk? The ad usually featured someone with a white "milk mustache." The ad then asked, "Got milk?" suggesting that if your answer is "yes,'" there should be some evidence like a white mustache or, more importantly, a healthy body.

Like our physical body needs milk, our spiritual body needs milk to be strong and mature. Peter's letter lets us know that we should long for this spiritual milk, which is righteousness in Jesus Christ: "Rid yourselves, therefore, of all malice, and all guile, insincerity, envy, and all slander. Like newborn infants, long for the pure, spiritual milk, so that by it you may grow into salvation— if indeed you have tasted that the Lord is good" (1 Peter 2:1-3). Got milk? Our desire for spiritual milk doesn't just happen. It requires a decision on our part. It requires us to get rid of behaviors and thinking that keeps us from living our best lives. For those of us who drink spiritual milk, we know its value and cannot live without it. This milk does not expire, and it is absolutely free.

Some people are spiritually lactose intolerant. They have digestive problems with the milk because they are used to drinking and eating products that are not good for them. They do not want to rid themselves of all malice and guile and other sinful behavior. But once a person is delivered from spiritual lactose intolerance, they will long for this milk. They will taste it, and see that it is good.

Often, we think one worship experience will deliver us, one prayer will do it, one day of fasting will suffice and one counseling session will do the trick. We go to church one Sunday and think we have paid our dues, but it is not enough. This is why many of us are stunted in our growth. We start-stop-start-stop-start-stop. Peter explains that for the spiritual milk to mature us spiritually, we must drink it regularly. Otherwise, we will not experience its benefits.

We need spiritual milk every minute, every hour and every day so change can take place, and we will continue to change. People who have spiritual milk see their imperfections as opportunities to become perfected. They see their problems as possibilities. They know every obstacle means an opportunity for growth and renewal. Got milk?

Like dairy milk, spiritual milk leaves behind evidence that it has been consumed. If Peter were doing an advertisement for spiritual milk, he might show a widow raising five children on one income. He might show a man walking into a drug rehab facility. He might show an eighty-year old running a marathon. He might show someone thinking about God's goodness, crying and shouting, "I got milk?"

Got milk? Yes!

When the walls seem to be closing in on us, when no good news is in sight and it seems things are getting worse, we need grace to help our unbelief. Jesus will make believers out of us.

Help My Unbelief

Usually, after a massive catastrophe, we hear heartbreaking reports of death and devastation. We also witness the struggle between hope and hopelessness. Then miracles happen. Rescuers find people buried under rock and debris, but still alive. These miracles make us believers. Jesus knows how fragile our faith is, and he provides us with signs to help our unbelief. We need to believe to have faith.

It doesn't take a natural disaster for us to stop believing in God's power. For many of us, as soon as something does not go our way or we experience a setback in our situation, our belief in God starts to fall apart. Be encouraged. Believe.

While Jesus, James, John and Peter were on the Mount of Transfiguration, a father brought his son to the remaining disciples below the mountain, believing they could heal the boy. But they could not. When Jesus returned and assessed the situation, he told the father, "All things can be done for the one who believes." Then the father prayed, "I believe; help my unbelief!" The father's faith healed his son. (Mark 9:23-24)

Often, Jesus cannot work a miracle in our lives because we do not believe. We feel so hopeless that we do not even pray for help to believe again. I visited a very sick woman in the hospital. She said, "I want to die tonight. I hope God comes to get me tonight." The dietician came into the room, taking notes on what the woman had eaten. She had eaten all of her dinner. I said to her, "With an appetite like that, you are acting like you want to live." She was struggling with believing and unbelief. We have all been there. We cannot get from not believing to believing on our own; we need grace. If we believe in grace's ability to help our unbelief, Jesus can work out our situations. We can witness a miracle.

When the walls seem to be closing in on us, when no good news is in sight and it seems things are getting worse, we need grace to help our unbelief. Jesus will make believers out of us. He does it by waking us in the morning, rescuing people hidden for days and enabling us to hear the testimonies of others who have survived their circumstances.

Jesus makes believers out of us by giving us strength to endure. Jesus will help our unbelief!

Many attempt to build their houses on cars, status, resumes and careers, but these things will not last. Only the things that we do for Christ will last.

How to Build a House

One time I baked some cookies from a box. I decided reading and following the directions were a waste of time, because I knew how to mix the ingredients and bake the cookies. The cookies looked good when they came out of the oven, but when my child bit into them, they were hard as rocks. I had left out an important ingredient—water. When we fail to follow God's Word and direction for our lives, we end up with a product that looks good, but not worth anything.

Jesus in his Sermon on the Plain proclaims his homiletic discourse in an area full of people afflicted with physical and spiritual diseases. Jesus opens with a series of blessings and provides hope of comfort, consolation and confirmation through knowing Christ and depending on his Word. Jesus moves quickly to the next segment of his sermon where he warns those who have found a false sense of satisfaction and contentment in the world.

Jesus' last point in his sermon consists of a list of dos and don'ts: Love your enemy, pray for those who use you, don't ask for money in return, treat others as you wish to be treated and don't judge. Jesus reminds us that in order to survive the storms of life, we must obey his spirit and his will completely.

Jesus closed his sermon with this parable: "I will show you what someone is like who comes to me, hears my words, and acts on them. That one is like a man building a house, who dug deeply and laid the foundation on rock; when a flood arose, the river burst against that house but could not shake it, because it had been well built. But the one who hears and does not act is like a man who built a house on the ground without a foundation. When the river burst against it, immediately it fell, and great was the ruin of that house" (Luke 6:47-49).

To build a house that will withstand the storms of life (criticism, rejection, addiction, financial despair, betrayal, loneliness, depression, temptation and tribulation), we must dig deeply. Digging deeply means reading and studying God's Word, attending Sunday school and Bible study, loving and praying for our enemies, doing unto others as we would have them do unto us and forgiving.

Jesus is the rock. Many attempt to build their houses on cars, status, resumes and careers, but these things will not last. Only the things that we do for Christ will last. We must take the time to follow the directions and guidance of the Word of God to survive the storms of life. We must be hearers and doers of the Word. When we express and build upon the love of Jesus in our hearts, we build upon the rock.

If we have faith that God has everything under control and has given us the victory, we can rest assured that we are equipped to defeat Goliath, even with a stone and sling shot.

I Got This!

We have all probably heard this inspirational story of God's willingness and ability to take care of our situations: "Good morning! This is God. Today I will be handling all of your problems. Please remember that I do not need your help. If the devil happens to deliver a situation to you that you cannot handle, do not attempt to resolve it. Kindly put it in the Something-for-God-to-Do box. It will be addressed in my time, not yours. Rest, my child. If you need to contact me, I am only a prayer away."

We daily meet the challenge of living a life pleasing to God, and turning over these struggles to God. Be assured. God is standing by and letting us know, "I got this!"

In 1 Samuel, we witness a battle between David and Goliath. The archenemy of the Israelites, the Philistines, paralyzed the Israelites with fear. The Israelites believed they could not defeat Goliath, a 10-foot giant. Goliath's height, looks and armor enabled him to intimidate the Israelites into believing they were defeated.

David, who had just been anointed king of Israel, explained to King Saul that although he was just a boy, he could defeat Goliath. David had defeated a lion and a bear with his hands, and he knew if God had enabled him to win those battles, he could defeat Goliath. God had already prepared David for this battle. King Saul agreed to let David fight Goliath.

With stones in his hand and a slingshot, David challenged Goliath, "You come to me with sword and spear and javelin; but I come to you in the name of the Lord of hosts, the God of the armies of Israel, whom you have defied.

This very day the Lord will deliver you into my hand, and I will strike you down and cut off your head; and I will give the dead bodies of the Philistine army this very day to the birds of the air and to the wild animals of the earth, so that all the earth may know there is a God in Israel, … the Lord does not save by sword and spear; for the battle is the Lord's and he will give you into our hand" (1 Samuel 17:46-47). David had heard from God, "I got this!"

Goliath cursed, insulted and prepared to kill David. Goliath thought David was a joke until one of David's stones struck him in the head and killed him. When we face our Goliaths, we need to know that the battle belongs to God. If we have faith that God has everything under control and has given us the victory, we can rest assured that we are equipped to defeat Goliath, even with a stone and sling shot. God requires us to rise to the challenge. God will take care of the rest. Hear God's voice saying, "I got this!"

Often, people see the worst in us, but we can always depend on Jesus Christ to see the best in us, just as he did Paul.

Jesus Saw the Best in Me

Plastic surgery is big business. Many of us have become overcritical of our features and are willing to pay big bucks to correct these "flaws." We seem to see the worst in ourselves. We do not have to engage in surgical procedures or any other treatments to be our best selves, because Jesus sees the best in us, and if we allow him, he can bring out our best.

Many of us are familiar with Paul's conversion on Damascus Road recorded in Acts. Before Jesus knocked him off a horse, Paul was Saul, and he spent most of his time persecuting Christians. In fact, the Scripture reveals Saul's presence at the stoning of Stephen. In his own testimony, Paul spoke about how zealous he was at murdering Christians. But despite Saul's hatred and murderous conduct of Christians, Jesus saw the best in him. Jesus knocked him off a horse, spoke over him, blinded him and gave him the grace to become one of the greatest apostles of Jesus Christ.

Saul's conversion to Paul shows that no matter how sinful we are, Jesus still sees the best in us. During Paul's conversion experience, Ananias wanted nothing to do with Paul because all he could focus on was the Saul in Paul. Ananias saw the worst in Paul. With some convincing, Ananias began to look beyond Saul and see Paul. Jesus said to him, "Go for he is an instrument whom I have chosen to bring my name before Gentiles and kings and before the people of Israel: I myself will show him how much he must suffer for the sake of my name" (Acts 9:15b-16). Often, people see the worst in us, but we can always depend on Jesus Christ to see the best in us, just as he did Paul.

Some people only can see us right now rather than the potential that lies within us. They point out the negative, never realizing we have divine destiny over our lives, and that we have changed. No one would have thought that Paul would preach, start churches, suffer beatings and imprisonments for the gospel and ultimately die for his commitment to Jesus Christ. But he did.

If we look at where we are now in our relationship with Jesus Christ, we may recall some skeptics, like Ananias, who thought we would never change, and as we were changing, they refused to believe it. But Jesus saw the best in us.

We must see the best in ourselves. We must believe that there is a best in all of us. Jesus will reveal it and bring it out, even if he has to knock us off a horse.

As we go through tests, trials and tribulation, know that God will not put more on us than we can bear.

Like Job

Most of us know the story of Job. During two exchanges with Satan concerning Job, God agreed to allow Satan to bring calamity over Job's family, finances and health situation. Although Job was an upright man, Satan contended that his obedience to God was based upon what God was doing for him, instead of who God was to him. After Satan destroyed Job's family and finances, Job still remained faithful to God. Satan, then, said to God: "Skin for skin! All that people have they will give to save their lives. But stretch out your hand now and touch his bone and his flesh, and he will curse you to your face" (Job 2:4b-5). Satan just knew that painful, disgusting boils would turn Job against God. God knew Job would remain faithful.

When we experience pain, Satan wants to turn us away from our faith in God. He wants us to get upset with God. However, the choice lies within us to give up on God because the pain is too great or to endure because God is so good! God is counting on us to make the right decision just like Job.

Like Job, we may be in a season of blessings and righteousness, and then suddenly experience hardship. Like Job, we must look at our suffering as opportunities to fulfill God's greater plan in our lives. Like Job, even though we wonder why bad things happen, we must remember that all things work together for the good of those who love God. The bumps and bruises of life, if we choose to allow them, can bring out the best in us and in God.

When we look at Job's situation, and try to imagine what he endured physically and the mental anguish from his friends and family, it is a miracle that Job came through this in his right mind and with his relationship with God intact.

God knew Job could make it. God had complete confidence in Job. Since Job came through with worship, prayer and praise in his heart, God gave him more than he had lost.

As we go through tests, trials and tribulation, know that God will not put more on us than we can bear. We, too, can experience recovery from our suffering like Job. Like God had confidence in Job, God has confidence and faith in our ability to remain faithful just like Job.

Once we realize we are worth being found, we come forth and make ourselves more available to the saving grace of Jesus Christ.

Lost and Found

At the end of the school year, the lost-and-found box is filled with lost phones, clothing, books, gadgets, and other items, which students have lost and forgotten. The lost-and-found is a lonely place to be. When we are in the lost-and-found of life, we can rest assured that Jesus will search diligently for us until he reclaims us.

To illustrate his love and desire to find us, Jesus told a parable about a woman who conducted a diligent search for one of her ten silver coins. (Luke 15:8-10). The woman knew that she had started out with ten coins, and when she went to count her money again, she realized one of the coins was missing. She lost the coin. However, just because the woman lost the coin does not mean it was her fault. Sometimes things get lost on their own. For example, we may put our keys on the table and someone else may pick them up, thinking those keys belong to them.

Coins have a personality of their own because they are relatively small and are subject to rolling around. The woman in our story could not simply backtrack her steps to find the coin. She searched the entire house for the coin. Many of us can relate to the woman in the story. As she looked for the silver coin, she probably turned the search into an opportunity to clean the house.

In order for Jesus to find us, he has to deal with our environment. After Jesus cleans up around us, we become more exposed and available to him. When Jesus conducts a search for us, he is really enabling us to find him.

The woman lit a lamp, swept the house and looked carefully. Jesus is the light. If we let him, he will get our house in order – sweep out the dirt and find us. When Jesus relates to the lost, he takes his time with them. How many times have we looked for our glasses and we discovered we were wearing them? Jesus does not overlook us.

Many of us write off people, sometimes even ourselves. We have fallen out of the bag and rolled around like a lost coin and have hidden behind a piece of furniture feeling unworthy. Once we realize we are worth being found, we come forth and make ourselves more available to the saving grace of Jesus Christ. Our worth is not in who we are, but in who Jesus is!

Jesus will find us even if we have been tossed in a lost-and-found box or rolled under a rug. We will testify, "I was once lost, but now I am found."

Although my grandmother knew that it would be only four people eating, she would fix enough for twenty-five. She just didn't want to feed us, but she wanted to fill us up.

My Cup is Running Over

Most of us have committed Psalm 23 to memory. It is such an important word of encouragement and assurance as we go through life to know that the Lord is our Shepherd, and we shall not want. David reminds us that the Shepherd does more than providing for our basic needs, but that our cups run over. God gives us overflow. When I was a child, I would eat at my grandmother's house every Saturday. She would have an abundance of fried fish and home fried potatoes. It was the best! After eating about three helpings, I would have to unbutton my pants to make room for more. My cup and plate ran over.

Although my grandmother knew that it would be only four people eating, she would fix enough for twenty-five. She just didn't want to feed us, but she wanted to fill us up. She did not want us to have to worry about only eating just what we needed; she wanted us to freely enjoy ourselves to our heart's content.

This is just not grandmother's thinking, but this is God's way of operating. God's desire for us is to experience all of his blessings. God's role as Shepherd means that God will protect us from our enemies and bless us in their presence. God anoints our head with oil. He blesses us. When God pours the oil on; God pours it on! God takes what we need and want to the next level; God makes our cup run over.

For our cup to run over, we have to make room for the oil. We have to empty ourselves so that we completely are open to the Lord shepherding us through difficult and challenging times. We must also be available to his rod and staff. We have to go where he tells us to go, and do what he wants us to do. If we follow the Lord, we will experience blessings pouring over in our lives even in the presence of our enemies. God will release the overflow when we release our will to him.

Like I made room for more of my grandmother's cooking, we will have to adjust our situations just to make room for everything God has in store for us.

My cup is running over. Let your cup run over.

Nothing just happens. If some things did not happen to us, we would not be the individuals God has intended. Our faith would not be as strong. Our testimonies would have less power.

Nothing Just Happens

We have lived long enough to know that nothing just happens. Everything we go through in life is connected to purpose and destiny. God is so wonderful and God's will is so powerful that even when we think we have messed up, God redirects us toward God's desire for us. Nothing just happens.

Ruth and Naomi find themselves in the middle of some difficult losses. They both have dead husbands, and in Naomi's case: a dead husband and a dead son. The mother-in-law and the daughter-in-law connect and move to Naomi's homeland. Even though Naomi believes she has nothing to offer her daughter-in-law, Ruth insists on going with Naomi: "Do not press me to leave you or to turn back from following you! Where you go, I will go; where you lodge, I will lodge; your people shall be my people, and your God my God. Where you die, I will die – there will I be buried" (Ruth 1:16b-17a). Subsequently, Ruth meets and marries Boaz and has a baby, who is part of the lineage of Jesus Christ.

Nothing just happens. Like Ruth and Naomi, we go through painful situations, including some we do not understand. There is purpose in whatever happens. If we are willing to recognize God's presence in all situations, we know that each of our experiences works for our good and for God's glory.

We have all been in Naomi's shoes. We have experienced deep loss, hurt and rejection and felt like motherless children. These feelings can make us question our existence and disturb any hope for a favorable outcome. We must trust in God. When I look over my own life, I recognize that my gender, race, having divorced parents, growing up in a trailer park, ending up at Fisk, attending law school at Emory, practicing law, answering customer service calls for a bank while completing a Master of Divinity at Vanderbilt, marrying, having children, divorcing and experiencing job transitions were not coincidences. They were designed to bring out the best in me, for kingdom building and to help someone else.

Nothing just happens. If some things did not happen to us, we would not be the individuals God has intended. Our faith would not be as strong. Our testimonies would have less power. We thank God, who has the power to organize pain and problems and turn them into divine purpose.

Nothing just happens.

God knows that we require restoration and repair to our spiritual bodies. God provided the best medicine for these aches and pains—grace.

Our Stripes Can Heal

Ebola, AIDS, cancer, and heart disorders are only a few diseases which have taken a toll on the human race. Indeed, our health is fragile. As scientists develop vaccines for diseases, we, as believers, must prophesy to and heal a spiritually sick and broken world.

The hope for healing is the suffering, death and Resurrection of Jesus Christ. Jesus' death on Calvary enables us to experience healing from physical diseases and illnesses that plague our spiritual well-being: "But he was wounded for our transgressions, crushed for our iniquities; upon him was the punishment that made us whole, and by his [stripes] we are healed" (Isaiah 53:5).

God knew that we needed saving from our sin as well as a Savior who could bring forth healing in our spirit. No matter how much we try to avoid hurt feelings, discouragement or rejection, things happen. God wants to heal us. God knows that we require restoration and repair to our spiritual bodies. God provided the best medicine for these aches and pains—grace.

There is no insurance required, and there is always the ability to obtain a refill. Our pharmacist is a loving Jesus who died and resurrected so we could experience grace. Each dispense of it has the power to deliver us from pain and people who hurt us. All we have to do is ask for it. As we experience personal healing, we can heal others.

The very sickness we thought would kill us enables us to bring life to someone else. Our stripes and suffering can strengthen others. Everything we have gone through – every disappointment, rejection, sin from which we have been delivered, death and tear we have cried – will bring healing to a hopeless and sin-sick world. Our stripes can heal.

As we grow in our faith, we must put our complete trust in God, who will provide for us in ways we could not do for ourselves.

Put God first

Do you remember the song from the Broadway play, "Annie," entitled "Tomorrow"? "The sun will come out tomorrow. Bet your bottom dollar that tomorrow, there'll be sun . . . When I'm stuck with a day that's gray and lonely, I just stick out my chin, and say, 'Tomorrow, Tomorrow, I love you tomorrow. You're only a day a way.'"

Many of us have experienced days that are gray and lonely. Annie is a good example of how to handle those days. We should stick out our chins and reflect upon God's promise of brighter days to come.

Sometimes what we are going through is so overwhelming, we cannot even think about the possibility of tomorrow. We have plenty in our lives to bring us down: finances, sickness, emotional pain, unemployment and love ones in need. The list goes on and on (the devil is busy). To avoid the stress and worry of tomorrow, Jesus gives us some guidance: "But strive first for the kingdom of God and his righteousness, and all these things will be given to you as well. So do not worry about tomorrow, for tomorrow will bring worries of its own. Today's trouble is enough for today." (Matthew 6:33-34).

These familiar verses are found in the middle of Jesus' Sermon on the Mount. Jesus emphasizes the importance of prayer, fasting, trust, and love. Then, he illustrates our human struggle with worry. He uses God's interaction with nature and one of the best-dressed Old Testament personalities to show us that we do not need to worry. God feeds the birds, clothes the lilies of the field and hooked Solomon up with some cool rags. What more will God do for us?

All we have to do is seek the Kingdom of God—put God first. Putting God first means finding ways to build up, fulfill and experience the Kingdom of God every day. Jesus understands that things in our flesh distract us from putting God first. When we become consumed with our physical needs (things we feel are in our control), we forget about the power of God, and we start to worry. Instead of focusing on the problem-solver, we focus on the problem.

As we grow in our faith, we must put our complete trust in God, who will provide for us in ways we could not do for ourselves. The clothing and food God has promised us cannot be purchased. We do not have to bet or guess whether the sun will come out tomorrow when we make heaven our goal every day! Put God first!

If we are willing to face problems and permit God to help us, everything will be all right.

Robin, It's Going to Be All Right

"Robin, it's going to be all right." I tell myself this often because, like you, I get overwhelmed and start to worry, fear and struggle over the possible outcomes of my situation. I have learned that everything will be all right and sometimes we have to remind ourselves of this theological truth. Jesus, who was about to endure horrific suffering and death on a cross, comforted his disciples with these words, "Do not let your hearts be troubled. Believe in God, believe also in me" (John 14:1).

We do not have to live with troubled, worried, fearful hearts because everything will be all right if we believe. No matter how wrong things go in our lives, if we trust in God's love for us, we know that after the dust settles, everything will be all right. We all wish we had a crystal ball. We could look into it and know the future. We would know exactly how things would turn out. The reality is that in this life, we do not have crystal balls to reveal the fate of a relationship, our marriage, our children, our health, our employment status or any other situation that makes us wonder about the outcome.

We seem to see conflict everywhere. We see people struggling with racism, classism and sexism in all forms. In our personal lives, things may not be going exactly right. Someone may be on the verge of a divorce, job loss, loneliness or financial struggles. It seems as though nothing is right. If we are willing to face problems and permit God to help us, everything will be all right.

The reassurance of knowing everything will be all right will bring peace and encouragement. If we just hold on to our faith, we will be okay. Sometimes, we get scared, worry and fretful over what might happen as a result of what we did or did not do or what is happening to us, but if we turn these concerns over to the Lord, he will make everything all right. We can still hear Jesus speaking to us, telling us "do not let your hearts be troubled."

Jesus is with us and promises that everything will be all right. It's more than feeling; it is a statement of fact: "Robin, everything is going to be all right."

We have had people investigate who we say we are and criticize the good we do, or even the suffering we endured. Talk like this can get us down, but still we can rise.

Still I Rise

My favorite Maya Angelou poem is "And Still I Rise." She opens with these words, "You may write me down in history with your bitter, twisted lies. You may tread me in the very dirt but still, like dust, I'll rise." The theme is that regardless of how one person puts another person down, there is still the ability and the power to rise.

This truth is also found in our Bible. Our faith teaches us that we will experience putdowns and oppression, but through Jesus Christ, we have the ability and the power to rise.

During Jesus' arrest and trial, people told lies about him. In fact, Jesus' accusers went looking for people who would tell lies on Jesus to put him to death. (Matthew 26:59). Rather than refuting their lies, getting defensive and debating the truth, Jesus remained silent because he knew he would rise. This should be our response when people lie about us.

We have all been the subject of someone's conversation. We have had lies told on us. We have had juries filled with people who do not even know us and haters who gathered to pass judgment with the sole intent of finding us guilty. We have had people investigate who we say we are and criticize the good we do, or even the suffering we endured. Talk like this can get us down, but still we can rise. No one or anything can stop us from rising.

People talked about Jesus during his ministry, and false witnesses rose up against him. We know the rest of the story. They wrongfully convicted

Jesus, hung him on a cross and watched him die. This happened on Friday. But early Sunday morning, Jesus rose.

In the end, we, too, will rise.

Still I rise!

If we find ourselves in the midst of struggle, we have the blessed assurance that our latter days will better than our former days.

The Best Is Yet to Come

Our best days are yet to come. No matter how good or bad are former days were, God promises us that the best is yet to come. Through Haggai, God prophesied to the house of Israel, reassuring them that although the newly built temple would not have the bells and whistles of Solomon's temple, its glory would be greater. "The latter splendor of this house shall be greater than the former, says the Lord of hosts; and in this place I will give prosperity, says the Lord of hosts" (Haggai 2:9). How could God outdo the glory of Solomon's temple? The glory falling on Solomon's temple was so awesome that it filled the place with its beauty and power.

The Israelites were concerned that the new temple did not look as good as the old temple, but God explained to them that what mattered was the glory – the awesomeness – of God's presence. God can top God. God can take anything to the next level, including how God blesses us and demonstrates love toward us. The more we worship and have faith in God, the more we will see that there is more to God than meets the eye. God keeps improving on what God is doing in our lives and for all of humanity. We may have it good now, but God is preparing something even better for us, if we are willing to believe.

If we find ourselves in the midst of struggle, we have the blessed assurance that our latter days will better than our former days. For us to realize this promise, we must remain hopeful, faithful and prayerful. The best is yet to come. People can testify to how they went through difficult crises with loss of a home, a job, a relationship or something they considered unparalleled, and then they saw God replace it with something even better. God wants us to have the best.

Manufacturers of computers and cell phones stay in business because they always look for ways to improve upon what they have done. Apple has spent time and money on research to discover ways to make their latter days better than their former days. Once upon a time, there was an iPhone, and now there is an iPhone 6. If Apple can roll out new products every year that take their inventions to another level, just think what God, our Creator, can do in our lives.

Get excited! The best is yet to come.

We are palm trees. When the storms of life come at us, we will bend, but we will not break. We are rooted deeply in faith, love, hope and grace.

The Palm Tree

Here are some encouraging words from David: "The righteous flourish like the palm tree, and grow like a cedar in Lebanon. They are planted in the house of the Lord; they flourish in the courts of our God" (Psalm 92:12-13).

This Psalm reminds us that no matter what the world is doing, we should hold on to our faith and beliefs, walk the walk, and talk the talk. David uses the imagery of the palm tree to show us that we are strong, resilient and prosperous because of our faith and belief in God. We are the palm tree, and we cannot forget this as we go through the challenges of this life. If we are rooted in God's will, we will flourish like a palm tree.

Palm trees are interesting. Regardless of how hard the winds blow or how difficult the storm, the palm tree bends, but it does not break. The palm tree has useful byproducts such as oils and coconuts. It provides shade and can flourish in the desert. It is an evergreen so its leaves never die or lose their color.

We are palm trees. When the storms of life come at us, we will bend, but we will not break. We are rooted deeply in faith, love, hope and grace. We also produce useful byproducts such as patience, self-control, love and other fruits of the Spirit. Most importantly, we flourish in any environment, even in a desert. When we need God's grace the most, our spirits are replenished with faith and trust in knowing God is with us, and God will make wet places in dry deserts.

We are tough and strong. No matter the season, our leaves remain green and alive. Even when we go through a rough season, our leaves will not fall off. We will look like we did in the summer when we are going through the winter. Let's hold on to our faith. The righteous will flourish like a palm tree.

We must see the bright side so that we can endure the weeping for a night and experience the joy the morning brings.

There is a Bright Side Somewhere

The Psalmist wrote, "Weeping may linger for the night, but joy comes with the morning" (Psalm 30:5b). No matter how challenging our situations, we must hold fast to our faith and trust in God. If we do this, we will declare with authority, that regardless of how dark it looks on this side, there is a bright side somewhere.

Many of us have been in the dark. We have struggled with sin, loss of loved ones, depression or hopelessness, and felt trapped in very difficult problems and decision-making. Those who have been in the dark can testify to how scary the dark side can get, and it can bring anyone to tears. To get through the dark, we as believers, must believe that there is a bright side somewhere. The dark teaches us some enlightening lessons. We learn that the darkness will disappear; day will come. Trouble does not last always. We also discover that we do not have to be afraid of the dark, because there is a bright side somewhere. Whenever we can grow and learn from a dark situation, even while still in the midst of it, we are looking on the bright side. The darkness challenged our faith, but the grace of God illuminated the bright side.

We must see the bright side so that we can endure the weeping for a night and experience the joy the morning brings. Often, when we experience shortages in our lives – shortages of friends, faith, money, joy or love – we focus on the bad. When we go through a spiritual recession, we must remember to keep looking for the bright side. Behind every dark cloud is a silver lining; it is always the darkest before dawn. We must continue to hope and endure because change will come. There is a bright side.

In a painting called "Hope," a woman sits on top of the world, playing a harp. The world is about to self-destruct. Nevertheless, in rags, scarred, bruised, bleeding and beaten, the woman plays her one remaining string on her broken harp. She has the audacity to hope with her last string.

Our remaining string is grace, and when we have the faith to play it, we see the bright side. We will be able to declare as the Psalmist: "Weeping may linger for the night, but joy comes with the morning."

Yes, there is a bright side somewhere.

We have to believe things are changing, even though they may look the same. We have to call those things that are not as if they were.

Things Are Turning Around!

Life's challenges and disappointments have the ability to discourage us, especially if they last a long time. Experiences shake our faith and make us question God's existence and God's interest in us. These negative thoughts creep into our minds and convince us that things will not get better. Be assured. Even though situations seem to worsen, God is turning things around for the better.

When we are down, the only place to go is up. We must keep the faith. From the beginning of time, God called things into existence that were not so, and we have the power to do the same thing. (Romans 4:17). While muddling through our problems and circumstances that seem never to change, we must speak things into existence, as if they were real.

When we are in challenging situations, God is turning things around. Do we believe it? How often do we focus on the negative rather than seeing God at work? If we lose faith in God to deliver and restore us, God can do all the turning around he wants, but it will not matter. For us to see things changing for the better, we must turn our attitude around. We must have faith.

We lose faith when we give our best and cannot see results. After constant trying meets constant failure, we start to think seriously about quitting. We cannot allow dreams or visions to fade away just because we lack the resources to move ahead or run into dead ends on our journeys.

We have to believe things are changing, even though they may look the same. We have to call those things that are not as if they were. This includes finances, job situations, wayward children and broken relationships. God desires to repair these things and even bring new relationships into our lives. Sometimes while God turns things around, some things are let go, so God can give us who and what is necessary to turn things around for us.

Even when we meet failure, we have to speak success. When we feel we have given all we can, we need to give more, knowing God is in charge. When we lack resources, we must allow our faith to take over, knowing God will supply all of our needs.

Things are turning around! Before things get better, they may get worse. God's Word gives us hope that even in the midst of the worst, we can still speak favor and deliverance as God turns the worst into our best. Things are turning around in our favor.

When we put all of our trust in God's plan for our lives, we will understand that no matter how complicated life becomes, things will work out.

Things Will Work Out

Some people live by the seat of their pants, while others plan every step of their life to the last detail. Both types of people often face disappointment because they go into situations with certain expectations, and they meet the unexpected. We must be open to God's plan of salvation and trust that things will work out.

When the Israelites fled Egypt, they had certain expectations, but things did not go according to plan. The unexpected happened on their journey. Pharaoh's army came upon them, and the Red Sea was before them. God assured Moses that they would make it across the Red Sea. God ordered, "But you lift up your staff, and stretch out your hand over the sea and divide it, that the Israelites may go into the sea on dry ground. Then I will harden the hearts of the Egyptians so that they will go in after them; and so I will gain glory for myself over Pharaoh and all his army, his chariots, and his chariot drivers. And the Egyptians shall know that I am the Lord, when I have gained glory for myself over Pharaoh, his chariots, and his chariot drivers" (Exodus 14:16-18).

God's plan was to make the Israelites understand their need for God. Even though our plans may be in line with God's plan for our lives, it does not mean that we have the power to determine how we will reach our divine destinies.

Sometimes God has another way for us to get to the place of promise. It may involve seemingly impossible challenges. Although we try to plan for the worst-case scenario, only God knows what lies in our path. When we put all of our trust in God's plan for our lives, we will understand that no matter how complicated life becomes, things will work out. Just like God parted the Red Sea for the Israelites, he will work things out for us.

Some people are grateful because God intervened in their plans. Some people rejoice that they did not marry the person they had planned to wed. Employees had planned to stay at one job until retirement, but they received a pink slip. Because of that pink slip, they could pursue God's plan for their lives. Some people were rejected, experienced a closed door and were ignored. But because they trusted in God's plan, they can testify that things worked out. We should be glad that our plans do not always turn out like we want because God has a better plan. Trust in God. Things will work out!

Eliab and others have been called. But you have been chosen. You are the only one who can fit the glass slipper of the grace, the anointing, God has poured over your life.

You Are Anointed

"Don't judge a book by its cover" is a cliché reminding us that what is on the outside does not determine the quality of what is on the inside. Samuel illustrates this truth through the anointing of David as king of Israel. Samuel, the prophet, arrives at Jesse's house prepared to anoint one of his sons to replace Saul as King of Israel. The first son who comes out is Eliab, the eldest. The Scripture describes him as tall and handsome. When Samuel sees Eliab, his immediate reaction is that he must be the one. Just as Samuel prepares to pour the horn of oil on Eliab, God says, "Do not look on his appearance, or on the height of his stature, because I have rejected him; for the Lord does not see as mortals see; they look on outward appearance, but the Lord looks on the heart" (1 Samuel 16:7). You can't judge a book by its cover.

Unfortunately, many of us react as Samuel did. We make determinations about people based on superficial attributes that have nothing to do with what is on the inside of the person. Eliab had the look – but not the heart – of a king. Many people may look as if they have been chosen to be the pastor, your spouse, the supervisor, the president, the employee, the coach or the quarterback, but they may not have the anointing to fill the position. God has not chosen or anointed them for the task.

After exhausting all the other sons Jesse presented, Samuel asks if there is another son. Jesse explains that he has another son, David, a ruddy, shepherd boy. Jesse does not think to introduce David because he thinks Samuel would not choose David. This mentality reveals how little we know or understand about God. We often overlook matters of the heart. Does she pray? Does he weep? Do they grieve over the poor and have a heart for the lost? These are matters of the heart. Because of this oversight, we often overlook our own anointing. We think we do not fit the mode the world wants.

So, we live a life tending sheep, rather than walking in our anointing. Eliab and others have been called. But you have been chosen. You are the only one who can fit the glass slipper of the grace, the anointing, God has poured over your life.

Stop allowing others to define whether you are anointed and selling yourself short. It is time for you to come out of the sheep pasture and accept the anointing God has already poured all over you.

You are anointed.

We can shake off things, people or situations, which fasten around us to poison our destiny and what God has in store for us.

You Can Survive a Snakebite

Poisonous snakebites are usually fatal, but we learn from Paul that we can survive the poisonous venom of the spiritual snakes that come to kill us.

After Paul and his crew survived a tumultuous shipwreck, they found themselves on an island. The natives cared for Paul and his crew. While Paul kindled a fire, a viper came out of nowhere, and attacked Paul. It wrapped itself around Paul's arm, but Paul shook it off, but not before it bit him. (Acts 28:3-6).

When the snake bit Paul, the islanders thought he was a criminal because the snake targeted Paul. The snake's intentions were clear – to kill Paul. The devil's intentions are clear when dealing with us. Satan's objective is to fasten himself around us, poison us, and kill us spiritually and physically. There is a solution. Regardless of how tightly the devil wraps around us to lodge his fangs into our skin, we can shake him off. We can shake off things, people or situations, which fasten around us to poison our destiny and what God has in store for us. We can shake off addictions, unhealthy relationships, depression and rejection.

After Paul shook the snake off, all eyes were on Paul. They were waiting for him to drop dead. To their surprise, he survived without any injury. Instead of thinking Paul was a criminal, the people now thought he was a god. We have power over the snake. It's not that we are a god; it is because we serve a God that gives us the grace to shake off snakes even after they have bitten us. We are inoculated with something that makes us immune from the snakebite. We are filled with the Holy Spirit and dipped in the blood of Jesus, which protects us from poisonous snakes.

Snakes are not exclusive to remote islands, they can show up on the job, in the church, in political systems, courtrooms, and other places to launch their attack. We cannot avoid snakes. They are everywhere, and like with Paul will come out of nowhere. What gives us courage is knowing that we are more powerful than the snake. As we walk through this life and encounter venomous situations, we cannot give up, because we can survive a snakebite.

Our feet are directly related to what we say and who we are spiritually. This is why those who proclaim the word have beautiful feet.

You Have Beautiful Feet

Feet have gained a reputation for being one of the most intimate parts of the human body. They also have the potential of suffering the most criticism because of their shape, size, structure and other issues such as bunions, corns and fungi. Regardless of the state of our feet, they enable us to walk, to run a race, to dance, to drive and to do other activities. However, our feet cannot take us anywhere that our minds have not already brought us.

According to Paul, regardless of how our feet look, they are still beautiful if we proclaim the good news of Jesus Christ. (Romans 10:14-15). Paul provides a simple formula on how to be saved. "Everyone who calls on the name of the Lord shall be saved. But how are they to call on one in whom they have not believed? And how are they to believe in one of whom they have never heard? And how are they to hear without someone to proclaim him? And how are they to proclaim him unless they are sent? As it is written, 'How beautiful are the feet of those who bring good news!'" Many people today have not believed, heard or called on the name of the Lord, and they cannot unless someone has been called and sent to preach to them.

The one who has been called and proclaims the good news has beautiful feet. "What does the mouth have to do with the feet?" Of course, we have all heard the cliché, "You put your foot in your mouth." If you put your foot in your mouth, you have said or done something that backfired on you. We have to be careful with our words because we might be the victims of our words and actions. Our feet reflect our faith and relationship with Jesus Christ. Let us not forget how the washing of Peter's feet alone purified his entire spiritual body. Our feet are directly related to what we say and who we are spiritually. This is why those who proclaim the Word have beautiful feet.

When our feet walk the walk that we talk, witness to the saving grace of Jesus Christ, and bring hope to the hopeless, regardless of how our feet look in the physical, the Word has shown us that we have beautiful feet.

You have beautiful feet!

Be Encouraged

Be Encouraged

A Hero Lies in You	141
A Life Pleasing to God	143
A Linen Cloth	145
A Living Testimony	147
Be Encouraged	149
Be Grateful	151
Be Persistent	153
Benefits of Prayer	155
Blessed to Be a Blessing	157
Break It Open	159
Dance	161
Encourage Yourself	163
Finish What You Start	165
Give God Your Best	167
Hallelujah	169
Have a Good Day	171
I Still Got It	173
I Want to See	175
I'm Hungry	177
It's All About Attitude	179
It's All Up to You	181
Jump into the Fire	183
No Weapon Formed Against Me Shall Prosper	185
Pray About It!	187
The Red Skirt	189
This too Shall Pass	191
To God Be the Glory	193
Under the Influence	195
Wait on the Lord	197
When the Praises Go Up	199
With God, All Things Are Possible!	201
You Don't Have to Live Like a Dead Dog	203
You Have Talent	205
Your Day Is Coming!	207

If we understand the ability of God's grace to overcome the effects of kryptonite, whatever was designed to take away our powers could actually make us realize that we are heroes.

A Hero Lies in You

When we think of heroes, we often think of superheroes from television shows. We may even think of firefighters or law enforcement officers as being heroes. They are all heroic in their own way, but we, too, are heroes. We possess super powers and we are equipped to do heroic actions. Sometimes heroes are unsung because they do not look like heroes, or what they did to save someone went unnoticed. Whatever the case, there is a hero in all of us. In John's letter to the church, he encourages them with these words, "Little children, you are from God, and have conquered them; for the one who is in you is greater than the one who is in the world" (1 John 4:4).

A hero lies in you! The hero is Jesus, who saved the world, protects us daily, rescues us from sin and delivers us from our enemies. Jesus' heroic efforts, working in us, makes us heroes. Although we cannot leap tall buildings, fly in the sky, shoot webs or dodge speeding bullets, we have the power to resist temptation and defeat spirits that seek to attack our faith in Jesus Christ.

Some people have heroic abilities in the natural, but fail to realize how powerful they are in the Spirit. All of us have been given some special ability, but instead of using our gifts, we allow them to remain dormant, enable the world to take advantage of us, turn over our destinies to others and permit the fear of using those powers to make us bury them. This is why some of us do not realize how great we are. We are greater than the world.

At times, we do not feel heroic, and we start to believe that the world is greater than us. Our enemies tie our hands, tape our mouths and blindfold us. This does not mean we are not heroes; rather, it means that we need God's grace. Often, we have to be placed in seemingly impossible situations to make us realize greater is he that is in us than he that is in the world.

Like Superman, we are all subject to some form of kryptonite. When Superman encountered kryptonite, he became weaker than a normal person. Kryptonite makes us tempted to stray from Christ: it can push our buttons; make us act foolish; or it can make us weak in the knees. If we understand the ability of God's grace to overcome the effects of kryptonite, whatever was designed to take away our powers could actually make us realize that we are heroes. God's grace is made perfect in our weakness.

Those of us who have discovered our super powers realize we are spiritually invincible. Heroes or "sheroes" never give up, because they know that in the end, they will win. Whatever we are going through in our lives, or how complicated things get, we cannot give up. We are greater.

A hero lies in you!

Pleasing God does not mean that we have to sky dive or jump from a cliff with a band around our waist; it means loving God so much that we are willing to live our lives without limits. God is pleased with our faith.

A Life Pleasing to God

How many of us pray, especially those who cannot swim, as we cross bridges that take us over deep, deep waters? Most of us probably do not think about the possibility of the bridge falling apart. We have an unshakeable expectation in the expertise of those who built the bridge and the materials used to sustain large volumes of traffic. Unfortunately, we do not live with such expectation when it comes to God's promises.

In Hebrews 11, the writer devotes almost an entire chapter to talking about faith and people who exhibit exemplary faith—the "cloud of witnesses." These people were not perfect, but they had faith. Embedded in these verses are these words, "Without faith it is impossible to please God" (Hebrews 11:6). Our goal is to have faith, and to be a member of the "cloud of witnesses" so that we can live a life pleasing to God. We must have faith in God and God's words just as we do with human-made bridges. We must do more than believe in God. We must put our faith into action, especially when we face challenges and crises, because in these times our faith is tested and strengthened.

Living our faith requires us to make decisions with the expectation that God will do just what God said he would do in our lives. When we operate in faith, our lives should testify to God's power, promise and purpose over our lives. Fear and doubt can weaken our faith as we struggle with living a life based on what we can see or one based upon hope and things not yet seen.

When we meet this struggle with faith like the cloud of witnesses before us, our faith will enable us to witness to God's power, and we will live a life pleasing to God. Pleasing God does not mean that we have to sky dive or jump from a cliff with a band around our waist; it means loving God so much that we are willing to live our lives without limits. God is pleased with our faith.

We need God's grace to have faith, and we need grace to walk in our faith. God does not require a great deal of faith, a mustard seed will do. When we please God, we will reap the benefits of our faith. He can do more than bridges and mortals can do for us; God can do the impossible. Don't worry about pleasing people or getting pleasure out of things, live a fulfilling life pleasing God.

The cloud of witnesses took their beliefs to another level by acting on something they could not see, hear, taste, touch or feel. We can do the same. We, too, can live a life pleasing to God.

For us to be dressed for the occasions in life when our faith is tested and our fears roar, we must be covered from head to toe with the armor of God.

A Linen Cloth

I remember my children fighting over a box of crackers when they were younger. My son had the box of crackers in his hands, and my daughter grabbed the box. He let the box go, but held on to the plastic bag which held the crackers. Elizabeth got the box, and Adric got the crackers because the crackers had another layer of protection. As we meet situations and people that try to attack us, we can remain steadfast, because we have an extra layer of protection—God's grace.

When the events of the Passion unfolded, everyone feared being arrested or even killed. Soldiers seized anyone they thought supported Jesus' ministry, but most of the disciples had run. The Scripture details that there was "a certain young man was following [Jesus], wearing nothing but a linen cloth" (Mark 14:51) He probably ran out of his house curious about what was happening around the corner and merely covered himself with a linen cloth. He had no idea of the danger he would encounter. One of the soldiers grabbed the man wearing only a linen cloth, and he was left holding a linen cloth watching a naked man fleeing for his life. The unnamed man decided that they could have the linen cloth, but they would not take him. It takes more than a linen cloth to follow Jesus. We need a faith that no one can strip away.

If we walk around with just a linen cloth, we will easily be chased away from following Jesus, or answering our call to do God's will. We will find ourselves easily discouraged. Simple things will have the ability to snatch away our faith—sinuses, a bad hair day, and traffic. The more difficult situations like abandonment, pain, and rejection will have the victory over us if all we wear is a linen cloth. Underneath the linen cloth is our nakedness, our weak and vulnerable flesh, and without something more to cover it, we will find ourselves stripped down to nothing.

For us to be dressed for the occasions in life when our faith is tested and our fears roar, we must be covered from head to toe with the armor of God. Then, when those things and people reach out to grab us, they will not have the power to make us run; we will be able to stand strong. Be encouraged. We have more than linen cloths; we have the protection of Jesus Christ.

When the blind man obeyed Jesus, he came out of his situation with this testimony, "Though I was blind, now I see." Not only were his eyes changed, but also his demeanor.

A Living Testimony

As we witness devastation in our world, the deaths of innocent people, the suffering of others and our own tribulations, we can become easily discouraged. We must also turn our attention to the many miracles happening all around us—impossible rescues, finding a good parking space at a crowded mall, and being healed of cancer. Big or small—Jesus is still doing unexplainable things in our lives to give us a reason to testify his power just like he did the blind man who was once blind, but then after an encounter with Jesus could see. We are living testimonies.

The Gospel of John records seven signs or miracles of Jesus Christ to reveal Christ's power and to keep us believing in miracles.   One of those seven signs is the healing of the man who was blind from birth. Jesus and the disciples spotted the man. Jesus noticed his suffering and, unlike the disciples, knew the source and the reason for his suffering. The disciples assumed that this man's sins had caused him to become blind. However, Jesus revealed that the man was blind for the purpose of being able to see through divine intervention: "Neither this man nor his parents sinned; he was born blind so that God's works might be revealed in him" (John 9:3).

When we meet challenges, we often ask, "Why me?" Why am I experiencing pain and suffering, financial struggles, loneliness, depression, backbiting and mistreatment when I have been doing the right thing – tithing, turning the other cheek, being a good neighbor? The blind man probably went through this same questioning, asking, "Why me? Why must I beg on this street corner?"

Jesus healed the blind man. He spat on the man's eyes and commanded the blind man to go to the pool of Siloam to wash out his eyes. When the blind man obeyed Jesus, he came out of his situation with this testimony, "Though I was blind, now I see." Not only were his eyes changed, but also his demeanor. No one recognized him. This is what happens when Jesus brings us out; we are different. The once blind man gained more than physical sight; he acquired spiritual insight.

Through our challenges, we can turn a "Why me?" into a "Why not me?" When we go through trials, God gives us courage and delivers us to be living testimonies for the world to see the power and goodness of Jesus Christ. You are a living testimony!

Sometimes we can be on a high and suddenly face a devastating low that has the strong potential of shaking our faith. Thank God for the Barnabas types who keep us encouraged.

Be Encouraged

Depression is a serious health problem in our society. Death, bad relationships, rejection, bullying, disappointment and low self-esteem can lead to a dangerous, lethal place if we cannot find a place of encouragement.

The early church experienced severe opposition, including persecution of those who preached the gospel. People feared for their lives, especially after the stoning of Stephen, one of the apostles. These early Christians were discouraged, and some of them left Jerusalem and went to various places to spread the good news only to the Jews. One group went to Antioch and shared the gospel with Gentiles. Many of them became Christians. This encouraged the people still in Jerusalem. The church in Jerusalem sent Barnabas, whose name means "Son of Encouragement," to the new Christians in Antioch, and he encouraged them in their faith. "When he came and saw the grace of God, he rejoiced, and he exhorted them all to remain faithful to the Lord with steadfast devotion" (Acts 11:23).

Although happiness and excitement encouraged the people in Jerusalem, they recognized the new Christians would face discouragement. The Antioch Christians were in the "honeymoon" period of their faith. They were encouraged. But Barnabas knew that their confidence and enthusiasm would be short-lived in the face of criticism and persecution. They needed encouragement.

Sometimes we can be on a high and suddenly face a devastating low that has the strong potential of shaking our faith. Thank God for the Barnabas types who keep us encouraged. They remind us through the

Holy Spirit of how our faith gives us the power to overcome negative circumstances, to rise above and to heal our hurts, and to find joy, even in sadness and defeat. They are the people who believe in our dreams and help us to accomplish them. God sends them solely to encourage us.

We cannot allow the spirit of discouragement to win. My teenage daughter, Elizabeth, participated in a dance contest with other fantastic dancers. She saw the level of talent and felt discouraged about her dancing ability. I reminded her that she cannot live her life measuring her gifts and talents against other people, but that she should continue to nurture and appreciate the gifts and talents God has given her. When one of the older dancers performed to my daughter's song, I knew she felt discouraged. I was not in a position to encourage her, so she had to encourage herself.

Sometimes we have to be our own Barnabas. We have to encourage our own faith. After the contest, Elizabeth was so grateful to have been a part of the program and to be among the ranks of some of the best young dancers in the city.

When we overcome the spirit of discouragement, we take advantage of God's will for us to walk in confidence and participate in life-enriching experiences.

Be encouraged!

We must be grateful. If we choose to be grateful, to give thanks in everything, no matter what happens in our lives, we will still have joy.

Be Grateful

One of our biggest struggles is our inability to see how much we are truly blessed. Being grateful is not easy, especially when meeting challenge after challenge, crisis after crisis and loss after loss. These times can make one ungrateful.

Regardless of the situations in which we find ourselves, we must "give thanks in all circumstances; for this is the will of God in Christ Jesus for you" (I Thessalonians 5:18). God does not desire for us to complain and lament what we lack or how someone hurt us. God's will for our lives is to give thanks in everything.

God is always blessing us in big and small ways to encourage us to give thanks. If we analyze our situation and are honest with ourselves, we would recognize that things could be a lot worse. We must reflect on what we have, rather than what we do not have. Many of us do not have a lot, and we have lost a great deal over the years – relationships, loved ones, money, jobs and even our health. However, during these hard times, God is still present and blessing us with life and the ability to overcome the pain and to recoup the losses. If we are willing to be grateful for what is left, God's grace will heal us and bring greater blessings into our lives.

We must be grateful. If we choose to be grateful, to give thanks in everything, no matter what happens in our lives, we will still have joy. This is why people in hospice, journeying through chemotherapy, bearing the responsibility of caring for loved ones and struggling through homelessness still bless God. They are grateful.

Being grateful is not attached to circumstances. Being grateful is connected to our love of God, worship of God and trust in God. God is always good, even though our circumstances may be bad. Our bad times can be good times if we are willing to give thanks in everything.

Be grateful!

Some, like the unjust judge, treat people unfairly because of gender, race, class or other demographics that have nothing to do with what God has promised in the Word. When this happens, we lose faith and hope.

Be Persistent

We do not have to look far to see injustice in our communities. We have also seen the scales of justice out of balance, but through the work of persistent people, things changed. There are "unjust judges," who deny people what they deserve as human beings, and what they have earned. These are not just judges who wear black robes. They are people who pass judgment on others unjustly. They are self-appointed judges who oppress and withhold power from the powerless out of fear and the need to maintain control.

In spite of unjust systems and people, we have to remain persistent with prayer. We even have to be persistent with God sometimes.

In the parable of the "Unjust Judge" (Luke 18), a widow pleaded with a judge to give her justice against her opponent, and the judge ignored her. Can you imagine how frustrated and upset this woman became? Many of us have been in similar situations when going to a bank for a loan only to be rejected, going to a supervisor for support only to be ignored, sharing problems with a friend who will not listen because she has problems of her own, or seeking comfort in a spouse who rolls over and goes to sleep.

We have been in this dilemma with God. We prayed for healing, deliverance, justice, joy, peace, finances, children, spouses, parents and other matters for years, but nothing seemed to happen. At first, we were like the widow, knowing that we were being obedient and faithful to God. We knew God would answer our prayer. Rather than our prayers being answered, however, it seemed as if things were getting worse or remaining the same. Unlike the widow, we did not stay on our knees praying, being persistent. We gave up. The story teaches us that God's delay is not God's denial. We must be persistent.

Although the widow was in the right, the unjust judge believed her status as a widow meant that she was not entitled to her rights. The judge, the person in charge of making sure people were treated fairly, ignored her complaints. Regardless of what society said or the judge thought about her, the widow still knew that she was in the right, and she did not give up. The unjust judge eventually granted her petition.

Some, like the unjust judge, treat people unfairly because of gender, race, class or other demographics that have nothing to do with what God has promised in the Word. When this happens, we lose faith and hope.

We must be persistent like the widow! If a persistent widow convinced an unjust judge, imagine how a persistent faith will influence a loving Jesus! Things change in our lives and the world around us because of our persistent faith. Jesus explained at the end of the parable, "Listen to what the unjust judge says. And will not God grant justice to his chosen ones who cry to him day and night? Will he delay long in helping them? I tell you, he will quickly grant justice to them" (Luke 18:6b-8b).

Be persistent!

To take advantage of what prayer can do for us, we must pray sincerely and acknowledge God's power to hear and answer our prayers.

Benefits of Prayer

Job applicants often ask, "What are the employee benefits?" Some jobs offer low salaries, but have great benefits. The benefits make the job worth the work. This is also true for prayer. Jesus taught his disciples how to pray, because he wanted them to reap the benefits of prayer. (Matthew 6:9-13) To take advantage of what prayer can do for us, we must pray sincerely and acknowledge God's power to hear and answer our prayers.

What are the benefits of prayer? When we are in a challenging situation, and we pray about it, we expect God to act like an email, a text message or a microwave oven. God's blessings often require us to wait. Through prayer, God gives us patience. Prayer speaks to our doubts and distrust and encourages us to wait.

Prayer also provides clarity and revelation. Each of us has been at a crossroads in our lives where we needed divine revelation to give us direction. Many of us have randomly chosen someone from the Yellow Pages to help us solve a problem. The Yellow Pages may help us find a mechanic, but that reference cannot help us to discern God's perfect will for our lives. We are completely dependent on the Holy Spirit to discern the bad from the good. We need to pray.

Through prayer, we can hear the Holy Spirit speaking to us so that God's will for our lives is clear. Like activation is required before we can use our cell phones, our faith requires the same. Prayer activates our faith. Prayer enables us to respond to God's amazing grace. God's response to our faith is healing, forgiveness, strength and deliverance.

Prayer changes things. We cannot change situations or people. We get into conflicts in relationships because we believe we have the power to change people. Pastors cannot change members; parents cannot change children; employees cannot change employers. Only prayer can make a difference in the lives of people and situations. God said to the people who are called by God's name that if they prayed, became humble and repented, God would bring about a change. No matter how challenging and messed up life becomes, even after we pray, we must keep on praying. We must PUSH (Pray Until Something Happens). God may not come when we want, but God is always on time!

The more we love our neighbor, the more God will bless us and enable us to be a blessing to others.

Blessed to Be a Blessing

Although many of us do not realize it, we are very blessed. The more we realize how good God is, the more we will experience opportunities to be a blessing to someone else. All of us are equipped to be Good Samaritans.

Jesus told the story of the Good Samaritan in response to a discussion with a lawyer over salvation. The lawyer asked Jesus how to inherit eternal life. Jesus responded that he must love God with all of his heart and mind and love his neighbor. The lawyer pushed the issue further by asking, "Who is my neighbor?" (Luke 10:30-37).

Jesus did not answer the question directly, but instead told of the encounter of a priest, a Levite and a Samaritan with a naked, beaten, half-dead man on the windy, dangerous road to Jericho.

The religious elite, the priest (clergy) and Levite (lay person) of the synagogue ignored the man. The road from Jerusalem to Jericho was referred to as, "The Way of the Blood" because it was so dangerous. Most communities have roads like that. Many people, including Christians, drive down those roads as quickly as possible to avoid seeing the crime, the drug-addicted, the prostitutes and other indicators of poverty and danger on these streets. Like the religious characters in our parable, we drive by as if these people are invisible.

The Samaritan notices the man because he views him as a person, not a problem. He has the resources to help the man because of his compassionate spirit. My neighbors, the Halls, have cut my lawn for a number of years, and shamefully, I have not paid them one dime. And they have never asked me for payment. With my busy schedule as a single mom, cutting the lawn is the last thing on my list to do, and they know how overwhelming my schedule is. I believe they do it out of compassion, care, and love. What a blessing! Jesus' story challenges us to reach beyond our next door neighbor and bless those who are different than we are and those who are on the road to Jericho.

We miss many opportunities to be a blessing because we put on blinders to the social needs and issues in our life. We pretend they do not exist or depend on someone else to fill the need. Jesus teaches us that our salvation is directly linked to how we treat each other, including the poor, immigrants, women, and others who may look and smell differently than we do. God blessed and saved us so we can enable others to be blessed and to experience God's salvation! Through the actions of the Samaritan – a person least expected to stop and show compassion – we recognize the church's need to improve its outreach on the road to Jericho.

The more we love our neighbor, the more God will bless us and enable us to be a blessing to others. With the words of Jesus, "Go and do likewise," be blessed and be a blessing!

The content of our alabaster box is mixed with worship, praise, pain and our deep capacity to love.

Break It Open

When I was a child, I had a piggy bank. I had saved up coins in the ceramic depository until one day I needed some money. It was painful for me to break open the piggy bank; there was no other way to access the change. Although today I cannot remember what I did with the money, I am sure that, being a child, that I wasted it on some candy.

In Mark 14, we witness the breaking open of an alabaster box filled with costly nard, a perfume worth a year's salary. Mary opened the box without hesitation and poured it on a dying Jesus. She knew it was time to break it open. People who observed this act of worship accused Mary of wasting the perfume on Jesus, and argued that she could have given the value of the nard to the poor instead. When others criticized Mary for her tremendous sacrifice, Jesus defended her. "Let her alone," he said. "Why do you trouble her? She has performed a good service for me. For you always have the poor with you, and you can show kindness to them whenever you wish; but you will not always have me. She has done what she could; she has anointed my body beforehand for its burial. Truly I tell you, wherever the good news is proclaimed in the whole world, what she has done will be told in remembrance of her" (Mark 14:6-9).

When Mary broke open the alabaster box, she opened herself for worship. This was no waste. We may not have an alabaster box filled with expensive ointment, but we have something precious to offer Jesus, which is meant only for him! The content of our alabaster box is mixed with worship, praise, pain and our deep capacity to love. Opening ourselves to people who do not appreciate us or abuse what we store in our alabaster boxes is a complete waste. It's just like wasting my piggy-bank money on some candy. The nard in our alabaster boxes is meant only for Jesus because only he understands and appreciates what we are doing and what we have gone through. Jesus is the only one who can handle the contents of our alabaster box.

When we do not give our worship and praise totally to Jesus, we miss the opportunity to experience the benefits: deliverance, forgiveness, strength, healing and a chance to express our love and gratitude for everything he has done for us. Giving ourselves away is a natural response to the grace Jesus Christ gave to us on Calvary.

Let us be like Mary. Let us pour ourselves on Jesus. Break it open.

When God restores our salvation, brings us back into relationship with him and makes his presence known in our lives, we will dance like David danced.

Dance

Many of us like to dance but are not very good at it. Some of us try our best to step to the beat, but some of us are dangerous on the dance floor, stepping on feet, flaying arms and elbows, and knocking people out of the way. Some, like me, are stiff and looking around to figure out what to do.

I have learned that, however a person dances, it is good for the soul. Dancing brings joy and is a way to express oneself. Dancing is more than the Electric Slide, NeNe or the Moon Walk, or The Whip. Dancing is living to our full potential, stepping out on faith and living our dreams. David danced when the Ark of the Covenant finally made it back to Jerusalem, the City of David. He danced and leaped in the air because God had reconciled with Israel and had approved David and the city worthy of the Ark of the Covenant.

"As the ark of the Lord came into the City of David, Michal, daughter of Saul, looked out of the window, and saw King David leaping and whirling before the Lord; and she despised him in her heart" (2 Samuel 6:16). He was all over the place. David danced until his clothes fell off. He was so caught up in the spirit; he probably did not even notice that he was dancing naked. Michal, his wife and the daughter of Saul, did not like the way David danced.

When God restores our salvation, brings us back into relationship with him and makes his presence known in our lives, we will dance like David danced. Something inside of us will leap for joy when we are in God's presence and when God makes his presence known in our lives. In no way should we be able to sit still, knowing how good and merciful God has been to us in spite of our struggles and shortcomings. When our favorite song comes on the radio, we immediately start snapping our fingers, rocking our heads, and tapping our feet. We should be doing the same thing when we think about God's goodness. We should be dancing.

Some will not like the way we dance for the Lord. They will not like the fact that we leap for joy when we praise. They will not like it when we step out on faith. We must be like David and dance, no matter what anyone else thinks or does. God is our dancing partner, and God loves undignified, no-limit, all-out, passion-filled praise.

Dance. Dance. Dance.

If we depend on others to encourage us, we will not realize how beautiful and full of God's promise we are through our relationship with Jesus Christ.

Encourage Yourself

One the most difficult challenges we face as Christians is staying encouraged. So many things discourage us from hoping and dreaming.

In the midst of these discouraging conditions, we must keep encouraged. Often we look for other people to encourage us – to tell us that we can make it, that we are beautiful and that we can do anything we want to do in this life. However, these people may not be found when we need a boost in our spirits. This is why it is important for us to understand that we have the power to encourage ourselves.

We witness the power of encouragement in the story of the woman who bled for twelve years. The account, in Luke 8 is framed within the story of a father seeking Jesus to heal his dying daughter. Both stories are replete with statements of attitudes of discouragement. Jesus' delay to heal the sick daughter, the crowd blocking the bleeding woman's access to Jesus and the people who laugh at Jesus when he goes inside the father's home to heal the dead daughter are all acts of discouragement.

The bleeding woman teaches us a valuable lesson: encourage yourself. Despite the crowd blocking her and Levitical codes prohibiting her from having contact with Jesus, she had faith. She thought to herself: "If I could touch the hem of his garment, then I will be healed." Jesus healed her. (Luke 8:43-44)

No one encouraged the woman; she encouraged herself. If we depend on others to encourage us, we will not realize how beautiful and full of God's promise we are. Waiting for someone else to boost our confidence could mean never stepping out on faith. No one may ever give us enough encouragement to do what we need to do. We have to encourage ourselves. We do not want to miss out on the opportunity to be healed, delivered, and made whole just because someone did not give us permission to do so.

We have the power to speak over our situations. We have the power to lay hands on ourselves. We have the power to pat ourselves on the back. We have the power to press through crowds and touch the hem of Jesus' garment. The more we encourage ourselves, the more we position ourselves to encourage someone else.

Encourage yourself!

David's words to his son speak to us today as we take on the challenges God has set before us: Have strength and courage in knowing that God is with us and we can finish the work.

Finish What You Start

Many people start tasks but do not finish them. We can identify with reasons why, including procrastination, lack of resources, the birth of children, financial hurdles. The list of excuses is endless. There are so many books that have not been written; great teachers who will not show up in the class room; and creative legal arguments that will never be heard; and soul saving ministries that will not touch the lives of anyone, because someone started something and did not finish it.

David, the man after God's heart, started building the temple for the people of Israel but could not finish it. God reassigned this work to his son, Solomon. David did not finish the work but the work would be completed. In passing the torch and responsibility to his son, David said to Solomon, "Be strong and of good courage, and act. Do not be afraid or dismayed; for the Lord God, my God, is with you. He will not fail you or forsake you, until all the work for the service of the house of the Lord is finished" (1 Chronicles 28:20). Solomon probably felt both overwhelmed and encouraged as his father made this announcement.

Many of us have had similar experiences. God has given us an assignment, and it seems so colossal that we become discouraged and fearful. As we become involved in the work, the task becomes more complicated and consuming because, instead of taking it one bite at a time, we attempt to eat the whole apple. David's words to his son speak to us today as we take on the challenges God has set before us: Have strength and courage in knowing that God will help us to finish the work.

Everyone has heard of the story of the Tortoise and the Hare. Hare spent a great deal of time outdoing Tortoise. He competed with Tortoise in areas he knew he would win. Hare ultimately challenged Tortoise to a race. Although Tortoise knew he was much slower than Hare, he agreed to the challenge. Hare, of course, maintained a lead throughout the race, while Tortoise continued to move slowly toward the finish line. Instead of completing the race while he had the lead, Hare took a break and fell asleep. While he slept, Tortoise crossed the finish line. Tortoise won the race.

Tortoise was not in the race to win, but to complete the task before him. To Hare's surprise, Tortoise won the race despite the odds. We must understand when thinking about our own race that victory comes in completing the task. As we reflect on the things we have started and have not finished, let us keep going like Tortoise. It is not the first who finishes, but rather, the one who endures to the end. Be strong and of good courage and act. Finish what you start.

Whether we have a little or a lot, it is not much compared to what God has given us.

Give God Your Best

Isaac Newton's third law of gravity provides that for every action, there is an opposite and equal reaction. This law applies not only to physical things, but also to the spirit. When we give God our best, God renders an opposite and equal reaction—often times more. The more we stretch what we have to give to God, the more God will give back to us.

God spoke this commandment to the Israelites, "Out of all the gifts to you, you shall set apart every offering due to the Lord; the best of all of them is the part to be consecrated" (Numbers 18:29). God expects us to give our best and nothing less. Often, we fall short in giving money, love, time and ourselves.

We give God what is left over. This is not the best we can do. Disobedience, fear and lack of spiritual growth prevent us from giving our best to God. Many of us feel that we don't have our best to offer, but we do. Whether we have a little or a lot, it is not much compared to what God has given us. We want to give our God, who has everything and can do anything, something because we love God for who God is and for what God has done for us. This expression of love is also an act of obedience and worship.

We cannot measure what we have to offer against what others have or material standards. When we give of ourselves, we give our best. Too many of us give our best to others and have nothing left for God, except a short prayer as we doze off to sleep or a couple of dollars to put in the collection plate. Even if we are at our worst in sin, our deepest in debt and our lowest in spirit, we can still give God our best. God deserves our best.

When we are willing to put forth our best, God will give us the best! The more we give, the more God gives us. God multiplies what we have given. Often, we do not recognize God's best for us because sometimes our best is not what we want; it is what God knows we need to bring out the best in us. God gave us the best when, more than 2,000 years ago, God sent his only Son, Jesus. Give God your best.

Praise is not about our circumstances; it is about what God can do and who God is.

Hallelujah

There is power in our praise. Often, when troubles come our way, our response is to cry, give up, get depressed and forget God's promises. Our inability to praise God even during our life challenges reveals our lack of faith in what God can do and has already done in our lives. We have to give God an "anyhow" praise.

Multitudes of those who were in heaven witnessed the triumph of Jesus Christ over Satan and the marriage of Christ to the Church. (Revelation 19:1-6). They proclaimed, "Hallelujah!" They praised God. This victory is the reason we can lift up a hallelujah, even when we struggle through life, because we know in the end we will win. Often, we are like fans at a football game. When the team is doing well, we are rooting for them, but when the team makes a series of bad plays, we yell at the players and even leave the game. When God is doing everything we want God to do, we have our arms in the air, shouting, tithing, and giving God the glory. Then, when we hit rough times, we get upset with God and even stop talking to him. Regardless of what is going on, we should praise the Lord.

If we lose our praise, we lose our hope of fulfilling our divine destinies, and we will not answer the call of God on our lives. Praise is not about our circumstances; it is about what God can do and who God is. Material possessions, our health, and the economy should not determine whether we shout, sing, dance or speak in tongues. Praise is about God. When God gets the glory, no matter what happens in our lives, we will shout:

"Hallelujah!" Praise cannot be taught in school like a history lesson or in a do-it-yourself class.

Because we were created to give God praise, praise is instinctive in our nature. I had a church member to whom I delivered communion for years before she died at age 101. She developed dementia, and although she could not remember my name, through these years until her death, she would say, "Hallelujah," at the conclusion of our visit. She had instinctive praise.

The church has become tamed, domesticated and too sophisticated for instinctive praise. Praise has turned into something that is rehearsed, practiced and processed rather than something that just happens when we reflect on God's goodness. Often, we think too much. What will other people say? Who is watching? What are we wearing? This has nothing to do with God. We need to praise on instinct. Our instinctive ability to praise deepens as we go through experiences that shake our faith and make us totally lean on God. Then we realize that power, salvation and glory can only come from our God. As we go through life's challenges, we will experience peace of mind, joy and faith to carry us through if we bless God at all times. Like my church member, whatever our state of mind, we can still shout: "Hallelujah!"

When life deals lemons, make lemonade, and if the monkey does not show, get an ape and have a bigger show.

Have a Good Day

We all have had bad days. We woke up on the wrong side of the bed, and had an attitude for no reason, or we were still hung over from yesterday's hurt and pain. Yes. We all have bad days.

I have had times like this. Instead of having a pity party, I remind myself: "This is the day that the Lord has made; let us rejoice and be glad in it" (Psalm 118:24). We have to speak against having a bad day. We can allow our humps in the road, crises and challenges to disturb our joy, or we can rejoice and be glad in it. If one bad day has the power to steal our joy, just imagine what it can do to our lives. We must constantly tell our flesh, which demands that we respond with self-pity, anger, despair, crying, worry and fear that God made today. We should rejoice and be glad in it! Choose to have a good day.

David, the psalmist, recognized that God made the day. Everything God makes is good. When we view everything that happens to us as something good, even though it looks bad, we can still rejoice and be glad. One other theological truth that David noted in the Psalm is that when we rejoice and are glad, our day can get better. When life deals lemons, make lemonade, and if the monkey does not show, get an ape and have a bigger show.

The devil means it for our bad, but if we are faithful we can see that God is working for our good. God's plan is for us to grow in our faith. The question God presents to us in this situation is whether we can rejoice and be glad. Can we still have a good day?

No person can brighten our day like God can. Often, we are too hurt and ashamed to share our situations with good friends, parents or spouses. They may not understand or they may be having a bad day and unable to give us the encouragement we need to have a good day. This is why we need God, who can turn clouds into sunshine and frowns into smiles.

This is the day that the Lord has made! Rejoice and be glad in it! Have a good day!

God gives us chances and opportunities just to prove to us that we are still in the game.

I Still Got It

Life is filled with many challenges, controversies, wins and losses, and although many come out of these situations, they do not feel victorious. They feel defeated, torn down, worn out, and they sometimes do not know that they are on the other side of their struggle. No matter how forces around us may make us feel as if we have lost everything, as if nothing is left, the truth is we still got it. God lets us know that we still got it. Jesus said to his disciples as he faced his death, that they would meet some challenges, but they would still have joy: "So with you: Now is your time of grief, but I will see you again and you will rejoice, and no one will take away your joy" (John 16:22). We will have some tough times, but no one will be able to take away our joy. We still got it.

God puts us in situations to show us that we still have power, skills, and gifts that can be used by God regardless of what we have been through or how washed up we think we are. God gives us chances and opportunities just to prove to us that we are still in the game. We will experience days in which we feel like we do not have anything. Simple situations like bad hair days, or more complicated circumstances like a divorce or feeling wrinkled and old, can make us feel like we do not have it anymore.

We cannot remain in these places, believing that we do not have it. If we stay in these places too long, we will start living without it, even though we got it. This kind of living leads to depression and living below God's potential and will for our lives. We have to believe that we still got it. The truth is, wherever we are in this life or what has happened to us, we still got it. This is why we see senior citizens matriculating at universities, running in the park, preaching, and writing books. They still got it, and they believe it. Our age, looks, gender, shortcomings, friends, or enemies do not have the power to decide whether we have it or not. We have to declare, "I still got it."

What we still have is our joy and faith in God. Regardless of what we go through in this life, nothing can take away the gifts and the power God has given us to walk in his glory. I still got it!

We must follow the once-blind beggar's example and demonstrate an unstoppable faith that keeps going, even when people and circumstances try to put it out.

I Want to See

When we really want something, we will act with determination to get it. God always presents a window of opportunity for us to seize the moment for a blessing and miracle to take place. All we have to do is keep the faith. This is the lesson we learn from the blind beggar, Bartimaeus.

The story of Jesus healing the blind beggar is recorded in all four Gospels. Mark's version of the blind man's healing identifies him as Bartimaeus, a man who stood at the city gates begging for money. (Mark 10:46-52). During this time, blindness was a common disability and was viewed, like most illnesses, as a social stigma. Bartimaeus suffered with a disability, and was a social outcast at the bottom of the socioeconomic rung. He begged to survive.

While at the city gate begging, the blind man inquired about the large commotion he heard and someone explained that Jesus was passing through. Immediately, his attention turned from begging for alms to a loud plea for mercy. Bartimaeus could not see with his eyes, but had perfect spiritual vision. He knew who Jesus was and what he could do.

One would think that the crowd might have helped him get to Jesus. Instead, people in the crowd wanted him to be quiet. They told him, "shut up!" Undeterred, the blind beggar continued to cry louder until he got Jesus' attention. Jesus asked what he wanted, and Bartimaeus said, "I want to see." Why does Jesus ask the blind man what he wants? Isn't it obvious? Doesn't Jesus know everything? The blind man's confession revealed his faith and focus on what he wanted from Jesus.

Often when we pray, we are not sure what we want Jesus to do in the situation or what we really need. Bartimaeus' confession enabled him to hone in on his specific desire: "I want to see." Jesus gave him his sight, acknowledging how pleased he was with the beggar's powerful faith. Many of us, like Bartimaeus, are blind. We may see with our eyes; however, we are blind spiritually and choose to beg for things that cannot give us sight. We must follow the once-blind beggar's example and demonstrate an unstoppable faith that keeps going, even when people and circumstances try to put it out.

Jesus is passing through right now! Let us turn our attention to the One who can give us spiritual vision and enable our faith to actualize the miracles we desire. Tell Jesus, "I want to see!" We will be able to have more than 20/20 vision. We will have the eyesight that enables us to see the unseen. Believe in the impossible. I want to see.

We have to deny our flesh, our hunger, and feed our spiritual body to prepare ourselves for spiritual warfare. This is why it is so important that we make fasting a part of our spiritual journey.

I'm Hungry

Every parent has heard this declaration from their children after a sporting event, school, or church—I'm hungry. We all have said this to ourselves, "I'm hungry." Our brain lets us know when we are hungry. Besides growling stomachs, we experience headaches, grumpiness, and dizziness. We need food to fuel our physical bodies.

Eating indulges our flesh, and this why Jesus, upon the beginning of his ministry, engaged in a 40-day fast in which he denied his body food. Even though it weakened him physically, it prepared him spiritually for the encounter he would have with Satan. (Matthew 4:1-11). We have to deny our flesh, our hunger, and feed our spiritual body to prepare ourselves for spiritual warfare. This is why it is so important that we make fasting a part of our spiritual journey.

When we think of hunger, we think of being hungry for food, but there are things and people for which we hunger, because like food, they satisfy our flesh. There are people hungry for drugs. There are people hungry for relationships. There are people hungry for attention. There are people hungry for power. There are people hungry to have their own way. There are people hungry to win. The hunger they are experiencing becomes such a part of them that they feel like they need it to survive. When feeling hungry gets out of control, people will eat and do anything to satisfy it. We are just not ourselves when we are hungry. In this case of hunger, a Snickers will not turn us back into ourselves. We need the manna that comes from Jesus. It fills our spiritual bellies, brings complete satisfaction to our lives, and turns us into the person God made us.

We need to fast from those things that we feed our flesh, and have a hunger for the Word of God, prayer, healing, deliverance, and wholeness. To satisfy this spiritual hunger, we have to give up those things that feed the flesh so we can permit Jesus to feed and fatten us. When the devil rears his ugly head, we will be able to rebuke him like Jesus did.

In the midnight hour when we get hungry, and it seems like we cannot make it, Jesus will provide healthy options filled with joy, love, strength, and power. Be encouraged.

Our problems in this life have nothing to do with money, people or resources we think we lack. Our issue is with our attitude.

It's All About Attitude

Apollos Hester's post-game interview, after scoring the winning touchdown for his high school team, went viral. Apollos shared his enthusiasm with the reporter about how the team won the game. He explained how the team started slowly in the first half, and that was okay, but they were determined to finish fast and hard. He spoke enthusiastically about how his coach encouraged the team.

"When you truly believe you're going to be successful," he said, "regardless of the situation, regardless of the scoreboard, you're going to be successful. It's a mindset. You can do anything you put your mind to. Never give up your dreams." What a great attitude!

Attitude shows up in our choices and actions. Preparing to deliver the Israelites, God had chosen an unwilling Gideon to fight the Midianites, a powerful army far outnumbering the Israelites. With God's help, Gideon recruited 32,000 people for the Israelite army. Rather than going through boot camp, God broke down the 32,000 recruits with other creative measures. Gideon made two cuts: 10,000 men trembling in fear and 21,700 men kneeling to drink from a river (Judges 7). He kept the remaining 300 who lapped water into their mouths like dogs.

God knew that winning against the Midianites did not require numbers or physical strength, but a winning attitude. Gideon's army of 300 defeated the Midianites. They won with God's help and a good attitude.

Our attitude will determine whether we accomplish our goals. Our problems in this life have nothing to do with money, people or resources we think we lack. Our issue is with our attitude. It's all about our mindset. Some of us, including Christians, have negative, self-defeating attitudes that have taken us nowhere, except around and around on a hamster wheel.

A good attitude can help win the game, no matter what the scoreboard says. Often, we allow what others say and our circumstances to keep us from living our dreams, healing from hurt or facing our mortality.

God does not want us walking around with a bad attitude – always complaining, finding something wrong with everything, giving up, living in fear or strutting around with our noses in the air. Like Gideon's elimination process, we need to get rid of those attitudes.

God reminds us daily that he will see us through the impossible situations. If the scoreboard leaves us one point short or with 300 to fight thousands, it will not matter at the end of the day, because we have a good attitude and God will be there to help us.

We don't have to walk around with an attitude problem if we will just smile and be grateful. Attitude will give us the victory. It's all about attitude.

We must open our hearts to the Holy Spirit. Our destinies are in our hands. Like a billboard sign reads, "The grind doesn't lie." Hard work pays off.

It's All Up to You

Some may question why others are progressing spiritually, emotionally, financially and socially while we seem to lag behind. We go to work every day, but when it comes to doing the work necessary to fulfill destiny in our lives, we find every excuse in the world not to do it. We need encouragement.

The proverbial writer states a cold fact: "The lazy person does not plow in season; harvest comes, and there is nothing to be found" (Proverbs 20:4). When we do not work toward our goals during the season, we cannot reap the benefits. Often, the blame lies with the one who did not bother to work or produce. What happens during harvest season is all up to us.

The verse compares our spiritual work to planting a harvest. There is a time for planting, and it is up to us to take advantage of that time. Planting time often occurs when we do not feel like doing any work, when we feel like complaining, or when we believe we lack the ability to work and depend on others to do the work. To get the energy and focus to do the work, we must open our hearts to the Holy Spirit. Our destinies are in our hands. Like a billboard sign reads, "The grind doesn't lie." Hard work pays off. Many of us avoid the hard work by working hard in other areas. We use children, housework, and other stuff to busy ourselves, which are important, but we use them as an excuse not to do the work God has called us to do.

One of my friends had shared with a church member her thoughts about writing a cookbook. Years later, the church member had published the book idea. If we do not do the work, God's work will go forth, and we cannot complain. We have good ideas, but we must follow through. It's all up to us.

For us to make manifest God's promises for our lives, to reap in harvest time, we must keep the faith and obey God's Word. Although God's love is unconditional, God's promises often require that we have faith and obey. We often listen to the blessing and miss the part that says we must follow God's statutes to reap the benefits of the promise.

Do you remember the story of "The Little Red Hen?" As the Red Hen is preparing bread, she asks several of her neighbors, who are also animals, for help. They are too lazy and selfish to help. After she bakes the bread, however, the other animals want to reap the benefits of her work and eat. The Red Hen says, "No." Harvest time came; the animals smelled the bread, but could have none.

If we do not allow God to energize us to work and live obediently and faithfully, we will be like those animals and miss out on major opportunities and blessings.

It's all up to you!

Despite our fears, we must jump into the fire. If we do not, we will miss living the life God wants us to live.

Jump into the Fire

A primary stronghold in our lives is fear. We are afraid to do many things because our fears control many aspects of our lives. Once we realize how powerful our God is and that God is in control of everything, our fears will disappear.

Some of our fears are honestly founded. My son, Adric, is afraid of dogs because a dog attacked him when he was smaller. However, his fear of butterflies, and my daughter's fear of bugs do not make any sense; neither does my fear of mice and rats, especially since I am bigger than they are. Everyone's fears are different. But Shadrach, Meshach and Abednego reveal that we should not allow fear to overshadow our worship and relationship with God. We should not permit fear to keep us from doing what God would have us do.

Exiled in Babylon, Shadrach, Meshach and Abednego refused to obey an ordinance issued by King Nebuchadnezzar requiring everyone to bow down and worship a golden statute. The king offered the three Hebrew men chance after chance to worship the golden statute, but they refused, knowing the consequences would mean death in a fiery furnace.

Although Scripture does not reveal this human truth, the men were probably scared out of their wits. But they did not let fear control their worship or commitment to God. Instead, they said, "O Nebuchadnezzar, we have no need to present a defense to you in this matter. If our God whom we serve is able to deliver us from the furnace of blazing fire and out of your hand, O king, let him deliver us. But if not, let it be known to you,

O king that we will not serve your gods and we will not worship the golden statue that you have set up" (Daniel 3:16b-18). They jumped into the fire.

Despite our fears, we must jump into the fire. If we do not, we will miss living the life God wants us to live. We will miss the opportunity to see the work of grace show up in the middle of our fires. We may fall into the fire, but we must never forget that Jesus is present; he will not let us get burned.

This is a message to those who have been teetering on the edge of victory and hearing the call of a dream. Jump into the fire.

When weapons form, we have the protection of righteousness and grace. No weapon will succeed in conquering what God has in store for us.

No Weapon Formed Against Me Shall Prosper

Weather has the potential to affect our mood. A week of rain can have a grave impact on our joy, if we let it. We have the ability to overcome the effects of a rainy day and other things and situations that have us feeling discouraged and defeated.

Fortunately, we are heirs to a promise: "No weapon that is formed against you shall prosper, and you shall confute every tongue that rises against you in judgment. This is the heritage of the servants of the Lord and their vindication from me, says the Lord" (Isaiah 54:17). The promise means that although weapons may form against us, they do not have the power to conqueror our happiness or steal our joy.

These weapons are not necessarily sticks, stones, guns, or knives; these weapons are the fiery darts of the devil. Weapons form against us when someone makes a rude comment toward us, we argue with a loved one or a friend, the person we are in love with does not love us back, or the "boo" turns into a boom. One cruel and dangerous weapon formed against us is gossip and lies told on us. These are all artillery to keep us from experiencing the best God has for us. They may hurt us, but they do not have the authority to take over the rest of our lives. God will take care of the situation and reveal the truth. We do not have to do anything. Be encouraged.

Many of us have seen movies in which there is a battle between good and evil. Then, the unfortunate happens, the hero catches a bullet and falls to the ground. We know how enemies act. They cannot help but to stand over the lifeless body and gloat in victory. Then suddenly, the person they thought they had killed rises and crushes them. What the hero's enemies did not know is that he had on a bulletproof vest.

People may see us lying on the ground after being attacked, and they may even think that we have died. After all that has happened to us, they may think there is no hope for us. She can never write the book now; she's too old. He will never go to college; he has poor test scores and no money. The twenty-year marriage ended in divorce; there is no way love could live there anymore. When we start to think like this about ourselves and our situations, we have to remember that no weapon formed against us shall prosper. We cannot count ourselves out. When weapons form, we have the protection of righteousness and grace. No weapon will succeed in conquering what God has in store for us.

Stay encouraged. No weapon formed against you shall prosper!

Prayer has the power to remove our problems, give us amazing strength to handle our problems, reveal the truth about our situations and point us in the right direction.

Pray About It!

We all run unto problems and challenges. Big or small, they have the potential to weaken our faith and make us feel let down and despondent. We may even run into a crossroads, wandering in circles, not knowing where to go as we search for an answer to what is next. Even some of the happiest times – the planning of a wedding, the birth of a child or a graduation – can present challenges. When we meet these situations, our natural impulses cause us to worry, become angry, get even, sink into depression or give up. All of this reacting creates more problems and an even more desperate need to pray. Prayer should be our first response when we need encouragement, comfort and reassurance.

When Jesus faced one of his biggest struggles, crossroads and moments of stress, he prayed. He prayed in the Garden of Gethsemane as he faced betrayal and crucifixion. If Jesus felt compelled to pray, we definitely need to pray about it. Jesus prayed, "My Father, if it is possible, let this cup pass from me; yet not what I want but what you want" (Matthew 26:39b). He wanted God to remove the problem; instead God, gave him the courage to face his situation. Jesus relinquished what he wanted and yielded to what God wanted. This is what prayer can do: permit us to trust in the divine will of God for our lives.

Prayer is like Febreze air freshener. Although the dirty dishes, smelly laundry and trash are still present, prayer takes away the effects of the smell. Instead of running away from it, we can deal with it. Prayer can change our situations. Prayer has the power to remove our problems, give us amazing strength to handle our stress, reveal the truth about our situations and point us in the right direction. God responds to prayer.

Prayer gives perspective. Before we prayed, the problem looked impossible. We thought about it, worried about it, feared it and believed we could not overcome it. After we prayed, we faced it and overcame it, just like Jesus did.

Let us not forget to pray, so that when the time of trial comes, we will be encouraged.

God will ask us to do some questionable things sometimes,
but if we obey him, we will find the red skirt.

The Red Skirt

Here is the story behind my red skirt. I have had a Tahari ASL suit for about ten years. It's red with ridges in the material. Unfortunately, I stained the skirt pretty badly, and forgot to pre-treat the skirt before sending it to the cleaners. I decided to wear it any how during the upcoming spring and summer months. Then, reality set in—I could no longer wear the skirt with this stain. I had thought, "What if I could find a replacement skirt?" Weeks later, a voice called me to go to Burlington Coat Factory, and while looking through the racks of mix-matched clothing, I saw a red skirt. My eyes widened, and I said, "This is my skirt." But I just knew it could not be my size, I folded back the tag, and it was an 8P, exactly my size, with a price tag of $7.98.

The scripture is true, "What no eye has seen, nor ear heard, nor the human heart conceived, what God has prepared for those who love him" (I Cor. 2:9). There are some lessons about this red skirt I want to share. First, God hears our thoughts. He knows our inner thoughts, whether they are small things like a red skirt or something big like the outcome of a doctor's report or a prognosis for cancer. God also shows us in small ways that he is able to work miracles. Those of us who shop at Burlington know that finding anything in there is like being on a scavenger hunt. The discovery of the skirt in my size was truly a miracle. The other lesson learned is if we just obey God in the smallest things, he will lead us to our destiny and promise. I went to Burlington! God will ask us to do some questionable things sometimes, but if we obey him, we will find the red skirt.

All of us have some red skirts that are stained and beyond repair. However, it does not mean we cannot move forward or that we can never wear the red suit again, because God has the power to replace the red skirt—things, people, relationships, jobs, and other damaged goods. The red skirt is just an example of the compassion and grace God shows each of us, from the red skirts to the comfort God gives us in our deepest times of sadness and discouragement. We have to praise God over the red skirt, because we know he can do so much more. The red skirt is God's way of saying—be encouraged.

As we journey, we will have some dark days, but we can depend on God to provide us with the strength and hope to get through those times so that we can experience the light of day.

This too Shall Pass

Life is filled with struggles, uncertainties and disappointments. Many are suffering with illnesses, joblessness and homelessness. Some have endured many challenges and letdowns over the years. It seems like trouble will never go away. The truth is whatever we go through, it will not last. The saying is true—trouble does not last always. This too shall pass!

What encourages me when I am going through a tough spot is to remind myself that this too shall pass. If we are willing to keep the faith and trust that God is watching over us during our season of tribulation, we will be able to testify to someone else going through, "This too shall pass!" It's not just suffering that will go away; pain and hurt will also pass if we are willing to heal. Then, we will find ourselves walking in our season of blessings.

The proverbial writer said it best, "to everything there is a season, a time for every matter under heaven" (Ecclesiastes 3:1). There is a time and season for everything, whether bad or good. We have the reassurance that when we meet life's challenges, they will not last. Circumstances will change, because there is a time and season for everything. This too shall pass.

As we journey, we will have some dark days, but we can depend on God to provide us with the strength and hope to get through those times so that we can experience the light of day. In the end, we will succeed if we are willing to wait, struggle, mature and believe. God is in control of the time. We have authority over our willingness to change with the times and to get through the various seasons of our lives.

Knowing "this too shall pass" gives us the ability to keep encouraged as we linger in those moments of discouragement. It also keeps us from surrendering to those voices in our head telling us to give up. Whatever our path, God will help us and enable us to move through each situation, even if it is getting through an educational program, paying off debt, a state of unemployment, or a place of disconsolation. The struggle is real, but this too shall pass. We have all seen the movement of clothes in department stores as the seasons change. In the winter, we can buy shorts, halters, and sandals. The reason we can shop for summer clothes in the winter is because the retailers know that a new season is coming. We need to start shopping. There is a set time for everything. Seasons change. This too shall pass.

Whether we have gone to the doctor, visited with a therapist or enjoyed a long vacation, God still must get the credit for everything good and every resource that brings us out.

To God Be the Glory

When words fail us, giving glory to God is always in order. To God be the glory! God's glory is his mighty presence with us and the reassurance of his love, whether in the midst of difficult or good times. God gets all the glory.

God's glory rested upon the tabernacle Moses built in response to God's instructions. When the glory rested on the tabernacle, it filled the tabernacle and had the appearance of smoke and fire. The glory of God penetrated the tabernacle, and prevented even Moses from entering it (Exodus 40:34-38). This image of God's glory references God's presence and power. When we experience God in this way, we should give all the glory to God.

God gets the glory in all of our situations, bad or good. When we experience healing, deliverance and restoration, we must give God the glory. Whether we have gone to the doctor, visited with a therapist or enjoyed a long vacation, God still must get the credit for everything good and every resource that brings us out. To God be the glory. Often, we want to give the glory to some person, place, thing or even ourselves; but the truth of the matter is God gets the glory.

While in divinity school, during my last semester I had not gone to class because I had a baby and was working as an attorney. The school dean called to let me know that there was no way I could pass my church history midterm exam and that I should drop the class. In tears, I told the dean that I would be taking the midterm and whatever happened would happen. My church history professor called me personally to let me know

I had passed his exam. Immediately, I shouted, "To God be the glory!" He said, "You should give yourself the credit; you did all the work." Then, I explained, "I could not do the work without God." God gets all the glory. When we experience his awesomeness, we cannot help giving credit to God in this way, "To God be the glory."

Even in times of suffering and disappointment, God gets the glory. He gets the glory because in the midst of tears, hurt and pain, we witness people still praising God; and as we unravel it, we see God's grace at work. This is the glory that filled the tabernacle. Sometimes, God will permit our personal pain to become public and impossible, so that when God brings us out, we and everyone around us will have to give God the glory. No one else! God is the only one who deserves it, and the only one who can handle it.

To God be the glory!

It is impossible to have an encounter with the Holy Spirit and remain the same.

Under the Influence

When we hear that someone is "under the influence," we automatically think that the person is intoxicated or high on drugs. When someone is under the influence of alcohol, there is usually slurred speech, an inability to walk straight, and redness of the eyes. Being under the influence of anything shows up in how we act, our speech, our walk, and in our eyes.

Paul warned: "Do not get drunk with wine, for that is debauchery; but be filled with the Spirit" (Ephesians 5:18). As we embark upon life's journey, we should take every opportunity to let the Holy Spirit fill us to point that our walk is different, our speech is different, and our eyes can see with clarity. We need to become drunk in the Holy Spirit.

When we are under the influence of the Holy Spirit, we can and will do things that we would not ordinarily do in our flesh. When we are under the influence of the Holy Ghost, we are not the same. It is impossible to have an encounter with the Holy Spirit and remain the same. Once we get the Holy Spirit, the Spirit of God on the inside of us, the things that we used to do and how we used to think will change. The Holy Spirit influences us to love, to forgive, to serve others, to walk upright and to believe in the impossible. The Holy Spirit speaks to us. The Holy Spirit also teaches, guides and encourages each of us.

Paul warns us not to get drunk with the wine of the world. The wine of the world is not necessarily spirits like Ciroc, Hennessey, or Bud Light. Paul is more concerned with evil spirits that influence us to operate in ways that are contrary to the will of God. They cause us to stammer and stagger. This kind of drunkenness results in destruction, unrest, anger, violence, hatred, and division. As we look around at what is happening in our families, communities, and country, we can see that the world needs to sober up.

When we are under the influence of the Holy Spirit, rather than cussing out someone who has hurt us, we can respond with kindness. When we are under the influence, rather than being ungrateful, we will give God praise. When we are under the influence, instead of having an attitude of receiving, we will have one of giving. When we are under the influence, our temptations and flesh will not get the best of us. Rather than thinking of ourselves, we will think of others. This is what happens when we are under the influence of the Holy Spirit.

Be encouraged. Let us renew our faith in God and be overcome with the Holy Spirit so that our influence can influence others. As we live, let us do so under the influence of the Holy Spirit.

If we are willing to be strong and let our hearts take courage, we will experience the grace of God while we wait. We will mount up like eagles, run and not be weary, and walk and not faint.

Wait on the Lord

Hold a glass of water with your arm outstretched. At first, it seems easy to hold, but eventually your arm becomes weak. The glass of water that was light suddenly becomes heavy. This is exactly what happens when we wait on God. At first, the wait seems like something that we are strong enough to handle, but as time goes on, we become weak. In these moments of weakness and vulnerability, the devil tells us to let the glass down because it is too heavy.

When Isaiah prophesied to the people of Israel, God knew that the people were growing weary in waiting for their circumstances to improve. Things were getting too heavy. We have all been there – waiting on God. Our patience grows thin, and we become discouraged.

The prophet still speaks to us today. "But those who wait for the LORD shall renew their strength, they shall mount up with wings like eagles, they shall run and not be weary, they shall walk and not faint" (Isaiah 40:31). If we rely on the words of Isaiah, waiting makes our spirits stronger. While we wait, God is maturing, developing, and preparing us.

Often we miss the blessings God has for us because we are unwilling to wait on God. We live in a society that wants quick bailouts and fast transactions; we want things to happen right now. Microwave blessings do not last as long as those God is cooking for us in a conventional oven. We need to wait on the Lord. Some of us are waiting on a new job. Some are waiting for doctor's results. Some are waiting to graduate from high school, college, or professional school. Some are waiting for a spouse. Some are waiting for the opportunity to make more money. Waiting does not mean that we sit around twiddling our thumbs. While we wait on the Lord, we should get in position and prepare for what will happen when the wait is over. We need to fold a white cloth over arm, just like a waiter, and serve the Lord until our change comes.

We have to ignore those negative voices inside our heads trying to convince us that God will not show up. God's delay is not God's denial. If we are willing to be strong and let our hearts take courage, we will experience the grace of God while we wait. We will mount up like eagles, run and not be weary, and walk and not faint. People wait for hours and even spend the night sometimes in bitter cold on Thanksgiving evening to get the best Black Friday deals. We need to wait on God with that same desperation and patience.

God may not show up when we want, but God is right on time. God's blessings are worth the wait and are more valued than the newest television set.

Wait on the Lord!

We invoke the power of God's grace by identifying what we have and praising God for it! When the praises go up, the blessings come down.

When the Praises Go Up

Can you imagine feeding a family of four with two fish and five loaves of bread? Jesus and his disciples did more. They fed more than 5,000 people (Mark 6:30-44). When confronted with the problem of feeding this large number, the disciples wanted to get rid of the crowd because they did not have enough money to buy food for them.

These disciples, who had just performed miracles, did not believe they had enough power to feed the crowd. What the disciples lacked was not resources, but faith. Jesus instructed them to seek what they could find in the crowd. The disciples returned with two fish and five loaves of bread. Jesus took the food, held it up to God and blessed it. Everyone ate, and there was plenty of leftovers.

We must remember in our Christian walk and our desire to do God's will, God's work always has enough resources. Jesus' prayer and blessing over the two fish and five loaves of bread reveal the key to unlocking the resources available to us. When the praises go up, the blessings come down. We praise God for what we have, regardless of its size, shape or color. Demonstrating a grateful attitude multiplies the things we need to serve God.

Many people have a mentality of lack in the spiritual, physical and emotional areas of their lives. They believe that they are not good enough, pretty enough, spiritual enough, anointed enough or rich enough to do God's work and be who God has called them to be. None of us has enough of anything, but those who are in relationship with God and understand the power of praise realize we need God's grace to bless and give us the increase. We invoke the power of God's grace by identifying what we have, even if it only amounts to two fishes and five loaves of bread, and praising God for it! When the praises go up, the blessings come down.

Praise is telling God that we love and appreciate God's goodness. If praise can turn two fish and five loaves of bread into an all-you-can-eat fish fry, imagine what praise can do in our lives!

When the praises go up, the blessings come down!

Today is our moment to let the world know through our walk, our speech and our drive that dreams come and that all things are possible!

With God, All Things Are Possible!

Many of us buy into the idea that we are limited in what we can do because of who we are and what we have. The way to make the impossible possible is to step out on faith and believe. With God, all things are possible!

One of my favorite Jesus statements is, "For mortals it is impossible, but not for God; for God all things are possible" (Mark 10:27). The things to which God has called us often requires a miracle. They are more than our human minds can understand. We often lack the resources to accomplish what God has put into our hearts, even if we are the richest people in the world. We still need the precious resource of faith, which is only possible with God. Through God's power, we can do anything.

A hospital displayed an advertisement for its healing services with the slogan, "Nothing shall be impossible." Billboards showed physicians praying, patients coming through surgery, patients who recovered from cancer and someone with one leg taking a golf swing. The hospital recognized that its ability to help patients came from a greater power: God. We cannot do the impossible without God, who makes everything possible.

Anything is possible if we are willing to believe. Often, Jesus wants to do the impossible in our lives. He wants to put us on the path to greatness and give us the power to be healed and to heal, to raise people from the dead or even to become president.

With God's help and grace, problems turn into possibilities, doors open and little becomes much. Today is our moment to let the world know through our walk, our speech and our drive that dreams come true and that all things are possible! We cannot let possessions, people, letdowns or fear stop us from believing in the impossible.

If we stop believing, it will be impossible to live the life God wants us to live. In the movie adaptation of *Polar Express*, an eight-year-old boy wants to renew his belief in Christmas. After a trip on the Polar Express train, he starts believing and he never stops. At the end of the movie, Santa Claus provides the boy with a bell without a tone, but it still rings because he believes. Although his little sister can hear the bell, his parents cannot; they don't believe. When the boy became an old man, he could still hear the bell.

The bell for us is faith in God. We need to hear it, no matter how impossible or difficult the circumstances get. If the bell ever stops ringing, pray and ask God to let it ring in your heart. With God, all things are possible.

Whatever we lost or caused us to define ourselves as a dead dog, watch God bring restoration and healing, just like God did with Mephibosheth.

You Don't Have to Live Like a Dead Dog

Have you ever felt like a dead dog? Have you ever felt hopeless, desperate, controlled by fear, hidden or inadequate? Most, if not all, of us have felt like a dead dog.

After David had conquered and destroyed the house of Saul, he inquired as to whether anyone was still alive in the house. He wanted to show compassion on any remaining heirs of Jonathan, his best friend and the son of Saul.

Ziba, David's servant, discovered one remaining heir who had remained hidden for several of years, Mephibosheth. Mephibosheth was lame as a result of an accident that happened when Jonathan and Saul died, and his nurse carried him away and hid him. David had compassion on Mephibosheth, who had been living in isolation and fear.

David assured Mephibosheth that there was no need to fear and that he wanted to help because of his relationship with Jonathan. Mephibosheth bowed and responded with these words, "What is your servant that you should look upon such a dead dog as I?" (2 Samuel 9:8b).

Why would Mephibosheth refer to himself as a dead dog? He felt worthless, like a misfit. He did not understand David's compassion on him, especially after having lived years in fear of being killed and suffering with a limp. He felt like a "dead dog." He felt useless, unworthy, and hopeless. He thought he would have to live his entire life like a dead dog until David showed up.

Living in isolation or walking with a limp are not the only things that can happen to us to make us feel like a dead dog. Rejection can make anyone feel unworthy, like a dead dog. Abuse of any kind has the potential of making someone feel useless, like a dead dog. Insults, including being called a dead dog, can make anyone feel like one. An unfaithful spouse can make the betrayed spouse feel like a dead dog. It is hard to spot people who feel like this. Physically they may be agile. They go to work, church, school, and even take care of their children, but on the inside they are feeling like dead dogs.

To overcome this feeling that Mephibosheth had, a person must accept God's compassion and love. This is difficult to do. Instead of being open and available to love, often the person has built walls and lived in seclusion for fear of being run over again. The truth is, God does not want us to live like a dead dog.

God will encourage. God will deliver. God will resurrect. God is going to show us that there is hope. Whatever we lost or caused us to define ourselves as a dead dog, watch God bring restoration and healing, just like God did with Mephibosheth. Be encouraged.

We need to be grateful for the talent God has given us, and watch God bless us with more. If we are faithful over a few things, he will make us ruler over many.

You Have Talent

Jesus reminds us often that we do not have to go to Hollywood to search for talent; each of us has talent. Jesus tells a story about three servants who were given a certain number of talents, or money (Matthew 25:14-30). The master gave the first five talents, the second two and the third one. Then he left. He did not tell the three what to do with the money or indicate when he would return. Almost instinctively, the first two servants invested their talents while the third buried his in the ground. Without warning, the master returned and demanded an accounting of the money.

The two who invested their money doubled their profits and were rewarded with more for their faithfulness. The third servant, who did nothing with what he had received, ended up with nothing. Jesus reveals in this story that the Kingdom of God requires us to invest what we have for God's glory. The plot of this parable involves distribution of wealth. Everyone did not receive the same amount of money. The servant who buried his talent did so because he received less, and he was afraid to do something with it. We learn from the third servant that wealth and prosperity have nothing to do with the little that a person has, but everything to do with how the person invests what God has provided.

Each of us has something with which to work. God has left us with so many "talents." We should use our money and other gifts God gives us wisely, as the first two servants did. Our doubts and fears have buried these talents in the ground. We need faith to use these gifts for the glory of God. We spend too much time looking at the people with five and two talents without realizing how much God can do with our one talent. We become just as culpable as the man who buried his talent. We need to be grateful for the talent God has given us, and watch God bless us with more. If we are faithful over a few things, he will make us ruler over many.

Be encouraged today while there is still time. Dig up your talents and use them to glorify God. You have talent!

God will handle situations in God's timing and method. We do not have to worry about it. God has everything under control, both good and evil.

Your Day Is Coming!

Life is filled with many challenges and disappointments, and throughout these struggles we need encouragement. We witness wickedness in our communities, country and world: human sex trafficking, rape, random killings, hatred, and strife. We have to keep in mind that our day is coming, and their day is coming. Even though it looks like evil has a big lead, just keep on living right, and watch evil fade like the grass and wither like the green herbs.

In Psalm 37, God's Word encourages us to hold on just a little while longer, because our day is coming. This day will bring us a revelation and the manifestation of God's promises. The Psalm opens with these words, "Do not fret because of the wicked; do not be envious of wrongdoers, for they will soon fade like the grass, and wither like the green herbs" (Psalm 37:1).

All of us, at some point, have permitted evildoers to get under our skin. We have permitted them to steal our joy. We have even spent time trying to respond to their evil. Some of us have found ourselves jealous and envious of evildoers, while we watch them prosper and move ahead. We do not have to think like this because evil will be cut down like the grass and wither away like green herb. The psalmist's words are important to our understanding of God. The description of the consequences of evil and the benefits of good show us that God is watching.

God will handle situations in God's timing and method. We do not have to worry about it. God has everything under control, both good and evil. Like in the movies, the good guy will win in the end. Superheroes never give up, even when the odds are against them; and in the end, they experience victory. This is also true for us. If we allow God to order our steps, live after God's plan for us and put our trust in God, we will see God's salvation.

Your day is coming.

Acknowledgements

Dr. Chestina Mitchell Archibald
David Bers
Mrs. Rose Brown
Scott Davis
Meekhal Davis
Rodney Caldwell
Rev. Olivia Cloud
Dr. John G. Corry
Shirley Corry
Barbara Dunlap-Berg
Rev. Brian Fesler
Dr. Fred and Vivian Fielder
Kerry Foley
Rev. Enoch Fuzz
Eleanor Graves
Mrs. Henrietta Hardison
Bettie Harris
Norman Harris
Geraldine Heath
Tammy Hines
Rev. Chris Jackson
Dr. Gloria Johnson
Tana Kimbro

John Kimbro
Adric Kimbrough, Jr.
Drs. Charles and Blondelle Kimbrough
Dr. Edith Winters Kimbrough
Elizabeth Adria Kimbrough
James Lewis
Chelsea Mae
Rev. Pamela Miller
Pat Mock
Chaka Moore
Kelly Motley
Jonathan Richardson
Father John J. Raphael
Thalia Townsend
Ludye N. Wallace
Janisca Williams
Delta Sigma Theta Sorority, Nashville Alumnae Chapter
Meharry Medical College and School of Dentistry 2017
Montgomery Bell Academy
Pride Publishing, Nashville Pride Newspaper
Scott United Methodist Church
Tennessee Coalition to End Domestic and Sexual Violence

BIBLIOGRAPHY

Aesop's Fables. "The Tortoise and the Hare." (1867)

Angelou, Maya. *And Still I Rise.* "And Still I Rise." New York: Random House (1978).

Anonymous. "Good Morning, This is God." Web. 12 July 2015. http://www.heavensinspirations.com/good-morning.html.

Apple. Apple. Web. 12 July 2015. https://www.apple.com/iphone-6/

Avatar. Dir. James Cameron. Perf. Sam Worthington. Twentieth Century Fox, 2009. DVD.

"Burger King Advertising." *Wikipedia: The Free Encyclopedia.* Wikimedia Foundation, Inc. 18 May 2015. Web. 12 July 2015. https://en.wikipedia.org/wiki/Burger_King_advertising

Clinton, George. "Ain't Nothing But the Dog in Me." *Computer Games.* Capitol Records, 1982.

"Empire." *Wikipedia: The Free Encyclopedia.* Wikimedia Foundation, Inc. 6 September 2015. Web. 6 September 2015. https://en.wikipedia.org/wiki/Empire (2015_TV_series)

Febreze. Febreze. Web. 12 July 2015. www.frebeze.com

Franklin D. Roosevelt, Inaugural Address, March 4, 1933, as published in Samuel Rosenman, ed., *The Public Papers of Franklin D. Roosevelt, Volume Two: The Year of Crisis, 1933* (New York: Random House, 1938), 11–16.

Frederic, George. *Hope*. 1886. N.p.

Galdone, Paul. *Little Red Hen. Little Red Hen*. New York: Seabury Press, (1973)

Got Milk. Got Milk. Web. 12 July 2015. http://www.gotmilk.com/

Hester, Apollos. "TWC News Austin: High School Blitz Interview with Apollos Hester." Online video clip. *YouTube*. YouTube, 21 Sept. 2014. Web. 12 July 2015.

Jakes, T.D. "Nothing Just Happens." Online video clip. *Youtube*. YouTube, 30 June 2013. Web. 12 July 2015. https://www.youtube.com/watch?v=iSbt04Mm2nU

"Liberty Mutual Insurance 'Humans' Commercial (London Olympics 2012 Ad)." Online video clip. *YouTube*. YouTube, 31 July 2012. Web. 12 July 2015. https://www.youtube.com/watch?v=zfyWct2FJBU

"Mariah Carey—Hero." Online video clip. *Youtube*. Youtube, 24 Nov. 2009. Web. 9 September 2015. https://www.youtube.com/watch?v=0IA3ZvCkRkQ

"Music City Miracle." *Wikipedia: The Free Encyclopedia*. Wikimedia Foundation, Inc. 9 July 2015. Web. 12 July 2015. https://en.wikipedia.org/wiki/Music_City_Miracle

"Six Million Dollar Man Into." Online video clip. *YouTube*. YouTube, 24 Feb. 2015. Web. 12 July 2015.

Spiderman II. Director: Sam Raimi. Perf. Tobey Maguire, Willem Dafoe, Kirsten Dunst, James Franco. Sony Pictures, 2004.

Saint Thomas Hospital. St. Thomas Hospital. Web. 12 July 2015. https://www.sths.com/Pages/Home.aspx.

"Scandal." *Wikipedia: The Free Encyclopedia.* Wikimedia Foundation, Inc. 3 September 2015. Web. 6 September 2015. https://en.wikipedia.org/wiki/Scandal_(TV_series).

SNICKERS®. "The Brady Bunch." Online video clip. *YouTube.* YouTube, 29 Jan. 2015. Web. 12 July 2015. https://www.youtube.com/watch?v=HPR3PB_VGVs

Strouse, Charles and Charnin. *Annie.* "Tomorrow." Web. 12 July 2015. http://www.stlyrics.com/lyrics/annie/tomorrow.htm.

Superman. Director: Richard Donner. Perf. Mario Puzo, Christopher Reeve, Gene Hackman, and Marlon Brando. Warner, 1978.

The Polar Express. Dir. Robert Zemeckis. Perf. Tom Hanks, Leslie Zemeckis, Eddie Deezen. Castle Rock Entertainment, 2004 DVD.

The Wonderful Wizard of Oz, L. Frank Baum, author; W.W. Denslow, illustrator. George M. Hill Company, Chicago, 1900.

"Vashawn Mitchell Turning Around for Me." Online video clip. *YouTube.* YouTube, 8 June 2012. Web. 12 July 2015. https://www.youtube.com/watch?v=ZzbKwcC-Xmo